Beyond Book Reports

Beyond Book Reports

50 Totally Terrific Literature Response Activities that Develop Great Readers & Writers

Michelle O'Brien-Palmer

illustrations by
Denny Driver

Credits

Educational Consultant: Lori Blevins Gonwick

Content Editors:
Suzie Fiebig, Teacher, Kirkland, WA
Suzie Fiebig's 2nd-grade students
Eileen Gibbons, Teacher, Rochester, NY
Lori Blevins Gonwick, Teacher, Kirkland, WA
Lori Blevins Gonwick's 3rd-grade students
Martha Ivy's 4th-grade students
Marci Larsen, Principal, North Bend, WA
Valerie Marshall's 4th-grade students
Ruby Pannoni, Communication Arts Resource Specialist, Harleysville, PA
Sue Parker, Teacher, Redmond, WA
Sue Parker's 6th-grade students
Mary Schneider, Teacher, Woodinville, WA
Dr. Katherine Schlick Noe, Professor, Seattle University, Seattle, WA
Joyce Standing's 5th-grade students
Japhy Whalen's 4th-grade and 5th-grade students

Young Authors:

Lissa Rubin, Kindergartener
Lechelle Lucas, 1st-grader
Terry Yoo, 2nd-grader
Steven Yoo, 2nd-grader
Nick Palmer, 3rd-grader
Erin Rubin, 3rd-grader

Brian Schnierer, 3rd-grader
Philip Sanchez, 4th-grader
Shannon Bovan, 4th-grader
Brandon Schnierer, 5th-grader
Juleah Swanson, 5th-grader
Kaili Ka'lua'hini'nui Jackson, 6th-grader

ISBN 0-590-76991-X

Acknowledgements

I would like to thank the following people for their support and contributions in the creation of *Beyond Book Reports*.

I am especially grateful to the children who kid-tested, edited and provided project recommendations, quotes and inspiration for *Beyond Book Reports*. You have all been instrumental in the creation of this book.

- •Thanks to Suzie Fiebig's second-graders for kid-testing forms and for your wonderful story map, Venn Diagram and puppet examples. I thoroughly enjoyed your smiles, hugs and help.

- •Thanks to Lori Blevins Gonwick's third-graders for kid-testing forms, great group feedback, story map example, and lively literature groups. I enjoyed every minute in your classroom.

- •Thanks to Valerie Marshall and Martha Ivy's fourth-graders for sharing your weekly literature circles. Your groups were pivotal in the creation of Chapter Five.

- •Thanks to Japhy Whalen's fourth- and fifth-graders for your straightforward editorial support. Many changes were made as a result of your comments.

- •Thanks to Joyce Standing's fifth-graders. Your excitement toward literature and learning is captivating. Your insightful comments and enthusiastic support were wonderful.

- •A special thanks to Sue Parker's sixth-graders for your weekly editing sessions. Your attention to detail and the responsible way in which you carried out your role as editors was very impressive. Your editorial comments and suggestions significantly impacted *Beyond Book Reports*. Also, the time and effort you spent conducting your "books recommended by kids" survey will help other readers to find their special book. Thanks to Molly Brown for your rainbow idea.

I also extend sincere thanks to those who helped in the production of this book:

To the young authors for your examples of how to fill out the various forms and their actual projects – Lissa Rubin, Lechelle Lucas, Terry Yoo, Steven Yoo, Nick Palmer, Erin Rubin, Brian Schnierer, Philip Sanchez, Shannon Bovan, Brandon Schnierer, Juleah Swanson and Kaili Ka'lua'hini'nui Jackson.

To the editors for your dedication and enriching contributions to this book – Suzie Fiebig, Eileen Gibbons, Lori Blevins Gonwick, Marci Larsen, Ruby Pannoni, Sue Parker, Dr. Katherine Schlick Noe, and Mary Schneider.

To Lori Blevins Gonwick for your support and great ideas as the educational consultant, to Denny Driver for your delightful illustrations, to Laura Utterback for your great genre ideas, to Gid Palmer for your editing help and to Gail Schroder for your fine detail work.

Thanks to Marcene and Robert Christoverson for your ongoing encouragement of my work, and to Evelyn Sansky, a special friend, for your constant love, friendship, and support. Also, thank you Gid and Nick – I love you both very much.

Dedication

This book is dedicated to every child involved in its creation.

Suzie Fiebig's 2nd-Grade Class

Samantha Arnold
Jessica Berg
Miriam Brambila
Amber Cass
Ryan Clark
Derek Cruse
Erin Dooley
Tim Denning
Jessica Dressen
Hassan Eisa
Jesse Fox
Christopher Freni
Aaron Gwaltney
Milad Ghazvini
Alyna Holden
Elizabeth Hughes
Paul Jones
Hallie Luginsland
Madelyne Martinka
Oleg Mastikash
David Moneymaker
Chris Otte
Aaron Schmalle
Danny Spurr
Jake Standley
Derek Voelker
Elissa Wildenborg
Peter Zanassi

Lori Blevins Gonwick's 3rd-Grade Class

Marisa Brambila
Andrew Burns
Emily Dean
Steven Demlow
Brien Dodd
Alice Fairbairn
Matt Fillmore
Justin Ford
Justin Frei
Ford Harris
Cynthia Hsu
Michelle Kay
Karla La Hoz
Eugene Litvin
Leah Moore
Jeremiah Nusbaum
Brandon Ohm
Brett Ortiz
Christian Polocoser
Robby Ricker
Seth Robins
Lindsey Rose
Taylor Shalan
Renee Stokes
Lynnsey Sturgeon
Miychell Vereeke
Isaiah Washington
Matthew Wood

Japhy Whalen's 4/5th-Grade Class

Rubin Beyerlin
Jessica Blanch
Shannon Bovan
My-Lan Dodd
Kasi Farrar
Rachelle Ford
Taris Graham
Kelsey Holt

Dawn Hoskins
Cameron Lomax
Sean Leverentz
Clayton Martin
Fala Mathly
Wade Miller
Carolin Puloka
Michael Ragen

Jon Robinson
Delano Rogers
Lo Chon Saeturn
Geoff Teeter
Lela Tyson
Victor Victorino
Alerenzo Webb

Joyce Standing's 5th-Grade Class

Zach Carver
Jackie Ciliberti
Mike Corby
Steve DeShazo
Mollie Durkin
Andy Fawcett
P.J. Gordon
Mitch Kearns
Blake Laabs

Emily Mack
Matt McMurrer
Brianna Risch
Andy Schneider
Katherine Spiers
Kirsten Thomas
Tony Volpe
Alexis Waite
Kristin Ware

Writing Contributions by the Following Young Authors

Shannon Bovan
Kaili Jackson
Lechelle Lucas
Nick Palmer
Erin Rubin
Lissa Rubin
Philip Sanchez
Brandon Schnierer
Brian Schnierer
Juleah Swanson
Steven Yoo
Terry Yoo

Quotes by Others

Tiffany Driver
Ed Lobdell
Tara O'Brien
Gavin Schroder

Valerie Marshall and Martha Ivy's 4th-Grade Class

Tina Acena
Devin Austria
Eric Anderson
Matthew Black
Adam Borchardt
Colleen Carbrey
Lynn Chealander
Heather Cochrane
Mark Crockett
Kristin Culleton
Brian Dailey
Katharine Dunn
Thomas Fowler
Ryan Frankland
Todd Hannant
Chris Hartsell
Laura Hernandez
Timothy Hood
Lauren Humphrey

Timothy Hood
Lauren Humphrey
Christopher Huson
Brandon Jaffe
Eric Karm
Brian Kim
Brian Macinnes
Bradley Marsee
Jonathan Marshman
Jason Mattax
Jessica Michelman
Ashley Milligan
Brett Norville
Daniel Paris
Brandon Poyfair
Tara Rooney
Stuart Rowe
Natalia Sanoja
Marissa Sawyer

Chris Shearer
Megan Stauffer
Kenny Steele
Mark Stracione
Michelle Theriault
Shana Thirtyacre
Cari Thomas
Brynda Vela
Jack Vu
Jessica Walker
Matthew Warren
Tori White

Sue Parker's 6th-Grade Class

Scott Blake
Jillian Bloxham
Dale Chhen
Molly Clark
Britni Curtis
John Denney
Kentaro Gates
Lisa Heppner
Josh Hightree
Leslie Jensen
Rei Kayabashi
Andy Kim
Gil Mazurek
Hanna Molmberg
Karen Seligman
Sheetal Shah
Christian Sindayer
Eli Steurich
Nate Weirbach

Table of Contents

Introduction 10
Foreword 11

BEYOND BOOK REPORTS: Chapter 1
Introduction to Beyond Book Reports . 13-15

I LOVE TO READ: Chapter 2
I Love to Read 18
About this Chapter 19
Genre Trees 20
Genre Tree Descriptions 21
Interest Sheet 22
Interest Sheet Example 23
Our Favorite Books List 24-30
Books We Recommend Form 31
Reading Idea List 32
Reading Idea List Example 33
Reading Record 34
Reading Record Example 35
Genre Sampling 36
Genre Sampling Example 37
Favorite Authors Sheet 38
Favorite Authors Example 39
Letter to an Author 40
Letter to an Author Example 41
Author Profile Sheet 42
Author Profile Example 43
Illustrator Profile Example 44
Favorite Illustrators Example 45

READ AND RESPOND: Chapter 3
Read and Respond 48
About this Chapter 49
Story Sheet 50
Story Sheet Example 51
Predicting Story Outcomes 52
Predicting Examples 53
Response Journal 54
Response Journal Example 55
Story Map 56
Story Map Individual Example 57
Story Map Group Examples 58-59
Retelling Through Drawing 60
Retelling Example 61
Retelling Aloud 62

READ AND RESPOND: Continued
Retelling Example 63
Retelling Through Writing 64
Retelling Examples 65
Prediction Comparisons 66
Comparison Examples 67
Comparison Sheets 68
Venn Diagram Example 69
Character Comparison Example 70

READ AND REVIEW: Chapter 4
Read and Review 72
About this Chapter 73
Giving Book-Sells 74
Book-Sell Examples 75
Book-Talk 76
Book-Talk Checklist 77
Book-Sell Self-Evaluation Form 78
Book-Talk Self-Evaluation Form 79
Book-Sell Buddy Review Form 80
Book-Talk Buddy Review Form 81
Remarkable Reviewer Reviews 82
Reviewer: This Book's Hot 83
Reviewer: This Book's Not Hot 84
Reviewer: This Book is OK 85
Pizza Reports 86
Pizza Report Examples 87
Bubble Gum Review Example 88

LITERATURE GROUPS Getting Started: Chapter 5
Literature Groups 90
About this Chapter 91
Book-Share 92
Book Ballot Example 93
Book Exchange 94
Book Exchange Notes Example 95
Starting a Book Club Circle 96
Book Club Starter Questions 97
Group Focus: Genre 98
Genre Starter Questions 99
Group Focus: Story Elements 100
Story Element Starter Questions 101
Group Focus: Authors 102
Author Starter Questions 103
Evaluation Tools 104

Table of Contents

LITERATURE GROUPS
Getting Started: Chapter 5
Continued
Evaluation Examples 105-106

FUN READING PROJECTS:
Chapter 6
Fun Reading Projects 108
About this Chapter 109
Reading Project List 110
Reading Project List Example 111
Bookmarks 112
Bookmark Examples 113
Puppet Characters 114
Puppet Character Directions 115
Character Report Card 116
Character Report Card Example 117
Story Cube................................... 118
Story Cube Directions 119
Story Quilt.................................. 120
Story Quilt Example 121
Character Mask 122
Character Mask Directions 123
Character Wanted Poster 124
Wanted Poster Example 125
3-D Setting Map.............................. 126
3-D Setting Map Directions 127
Advertise-a-Book Poster 128
Book Poster Example 129
Project Supply Sheet Example 130

REFERENCE BOOKS: Chapter 7
Reference Books 132

FORMS TO COPY: Chapter 8
Interest Sheet 134
Reading Idea List............................ 135
Reading Record 136
Genre Pizza Toppings 137
Favorite Authors Sheet 138
Author Profile 139
Illustrator Profile......................... 140
My Favorite Illustrators 141
Story Sheet................................. 142
Story Map 143

FORMS TO COPY: Chapter 8
Continued
Venn Diagram 144
Character Comparison Sheet 145
Remarkable Reviewer Forms 146-148
Pizza Reports 149-150
Bubble Gum Review 151
Book Ballot and Book Exchange Notes .. 152
Group Self-Evaluation Form 153
Group Leader Record Keeping Form 154
Reading Project List 155
Bookmark Templates 156
Character Report Card 157
Project Supply Sheets....................... 158

Introduction

BEYOND BOOK REPORTS: 50 Totally Terrific Literature Response Activities That Develop Great Readers and Writers is written to help children (2nd-6th grade) become lifelong readers, forever *hooked-on-books*.

In this pursuit, *Beyond Book Reports* emphasizes respect for the reader's choice of book and his or her unique response to literature. It is intended to promote thoughtful analysis of what has been read and to validate a reader's experience through open-ended, thought-provoking questions. As sharing is an enriching experience for all involved, *Beyond Book Reports* is written to encourage the reader to share his/her insights into literature through various individual reading projects as well as in nurturing, relaxed literature circles or groups. But most of all, *Beyond Book Reports* is about the joy and exhilaration that comes from reading and sharing one's literature experience.

Although the text speaks to the young reader directly, it will require adult supervision and guidance in most cases. Many chapters include a page defining the main topic and a page giving information about their contents. Whenever more information might be helpful to parents or teachers it will be found in italics just under the top border of a text page. The second chapter (I Love to Read) includes a list of books recommended by kids. It does not reflect the author's reading recommendations or grade level appropriateness. It reflects the children's uncensored list of the books they love to read. If you are interested in a book list recommended by adults, there are many lists available at your local library. There is also a chapter of forms for you to use with your readers at school or home. Make as many copies of these forms as you need. The resource chapter at the end of the book is intended to provide a list of excellent reference books for bringing literature into the classroom or home. I highly recommend these books.

Each idea in this book is meant to be taken as liberally as possible. There is no one right way to do anything. The more variations created, the more exciting the process will be.

Guide, listen and experience each young reader's unique response to literature!

Foreword: Note to Kids

"When I read books I learn about people like George Washington and Abraham Lincoln, and go on adventures in my mind."

Tara O'Brien,
2nd grade

"If when I'm reading I put my feelings inside the story, I know it's a good book!"

Michelle Kay,
3rd grade

"When I read I feel warm and it has my full attention. I am in the book like I 'm my favorite character."

Steven DeShazo,
5th grade

I love to read. When I read a book I can experience different worlds just like the kids in the quotes. A great book takes me on incredible adventures. I enjoy imagining the characters and setting as the author's words paint pictures in my mind.

As I've travelled to many different classrooms and talked with kids about books, I've found that kids love books too. The kids in these classrooms were having so much fun reading that I decided to write a book to share their favorite reading experiences with you. I have included some of their favorite books in *Beyond Book Reports*. See if there are some you've read and others you might be interested in reading. You will also find their recommendations for a variety of fun reading projects and creative ways to share your reading experience with others.

I wish you many wonderful reading adventures!

Chapter 1

Introduction

Introduction to Beyond Book Reports

This chapter provides a brief introduction to each chapter. For more detailed information please see the actual chapter. The text was written with the help of over 150 children. They were part of the writing and editing process from start to finish. The young authors who share their unedited examples of various graphic organizers and reading projects in the book are listed below:

Shannon Bovan
Kaili Jackson
Lechelle Lucas
Nick Palmer
Erin Rubin
Lissa Rubin
Philip Sanchez
Brandon Schnierer
Brian Schnierer
Juleah Swanson
Steven Yoo
Terry Yoo

Illustrations:

The illustrations in this book were selected for their thought-provoking abilities. As in reading, each person will experience the illustrations in their own unique way. The children involved in the creation of this text had fun discussing what they saw in each illustration.

Chapter 2: I Love to Read

This chapter is intended to help readers determine their reading interests, including topic and genre, and help them select their own special book. They are encouraged to list the books they may wish to read in the future and record books as they read them. Readers will find fun ways to write to favorite authors and illustrators, and share this information with their friends.

Chapter 3: Read and Respond

Each person experiences a book in a unique way. This chapter suggests a number of ways readers can respond to literature. There are examples of a response journal, story predictions, story maps, retelling stories and comparing and contrasting literature. Readers are encouraged to share their literature experience with others.

Chapter 4: Read and Review

As we experience the book we are reading, we also evaluate its meaning to us. If it is interesting we keep reading. If it isn't, we lose interest. Read and Review is a chapter which explores fun, exciting ways to review a book. Ideas range from Book-Sells to Pizza Reviews. They are all highly recommended by kids.

Chapter 5: Literature Groups (Getting Started)

A natural way of sharing books is to form literature groups. Younger readers seem to enjoy very small groups of five members or less. Even in the 6th-grade, seven seems to be an ideal number of group members. This chapter is dedicated to helping you form literature groups in your classroom or home. Therefore, a number of group focus ideas have been presented.

Chapter 6: Fun Reading Projects

The excitement of reading a good book is wonderful. This chapter provides projects recommended by kids. These projects are fun and help readers synthesize and apply what they have learned from the books they have read. Each project is kid-tested and approved. Readers will find a project checklist and supply form to help organize their projects.

Chapter 7: Reference Books

This chapter contains a list of additional professional resources.

Chapter 8: Reproducible Graphic Organizers

This chapter contains all the reproducible graphic organizers and forms you and your students will need to complete the activities throughout this book.

Have fun reading!

Chapter 2

I Love to Read

I Love to Read

"I love to read because you become more involved with the story. You feel more for the characters than you would watching the story on TV." Jackie Ciliberti, 5th grade

Reading can take us into unknown worlds: past the barriers, boundaries and limitations of our bodies and life experience. A book can tug at our emotions, making us laugh, cry, scream or shout. It can extend our perceptions of this world and stimulate our imaginations as we enter fantastic new worlds never dreamed of before. When we select <u>our</u> own books and follow <u>our</u> interests, reading becomes a lifelong passion.

This is an especially fun chapter. It helps you determine your interests, select a book, write to your favorite authors and illustrators, and keep track of your reading. This is a time to think about what you like to read and whose books you like to read. Share your ideas with your friends. ***A book is a wonderful gift to share.***

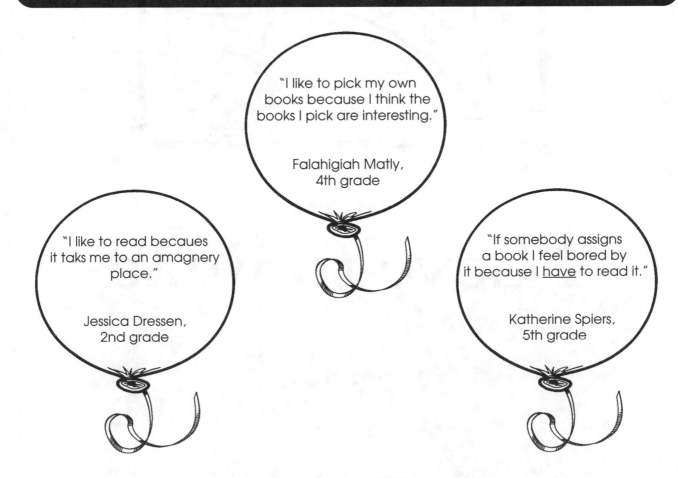

"I like to pick my own books because I think the books I pick are interesting."

Falahigiah Matly,
4th grade

"I like to read becaues it taks me to an amagnery place."

Jessica Dressen,
2nd grade

"If somebody assigns a book I feel bored by it because I <u>have</u> to read it."

Katherine Spiers,
5th grade

About This Chapter

This chapter includes...

Book Selection

Readers select a book in many different ways.

Genre Trees
Page 20

overview of different types of books (fiction and nonfiction)

Interest Sheet
Page 22

younger readers list their interests and select a book with help

Favorite Books List
Page 24-31

students at an elementary school recommend their favorite books to help others find a book
write your recommendations on page 31

Reading Idea List
Page 32

readers list books they may want to read in the future

Reading Record
Page 34

readers keep track of their reading

Genre Sampling
Page 36

pizza lovers read their way toward a yummy pizza as they sample various genres

Book Sharing

Readers can share their favorite authors and illustrators with others.

Favorite Author
Page 39

exciting cloudbursts to list favorite authors and their books

Favorite Illustrator
Page 45

star-studded rainbows to list favorite illustrators and their books

Write a Letter
Page 40

ideas on how to write a letter to a favorite author/illustrator

Author Profile
Page 42

clipboard and file folders to record information about an author

Illustrator Profile
Page 44

paint drops and easels to record information about an illustrator

Genre Trees
Different Types of Books

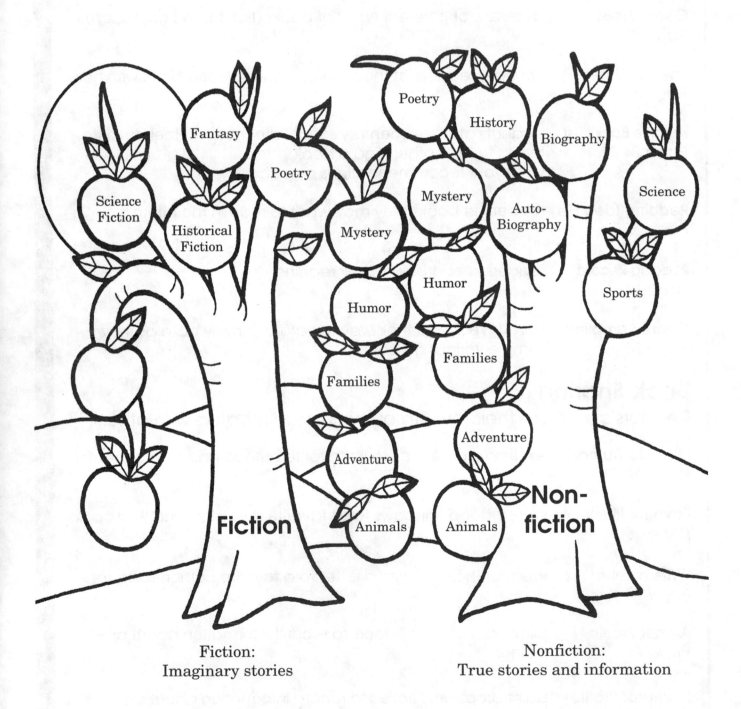

Science Fiction
Fantasy
Poetry
Historical Fiction
Poetry
Mystery
History
Biography
Mystery
Auto-Biography
Science
Humor
Humor
Sports
Families
Families
Adventure
Adventure
Fiction
Animals
Animals
Non-fiction

Fiction:
Imaginary stories

Nonfiction:
True stories and information

Genre Tree Descriptions

Fiction

Adventure
- Exciting imaginary journeys to interesting places
- Can include spies
- Stories present obstacles

Historical Fiction
- Stories of imaginary people based upon historical events
- Made-up stories based upon real people

Mystery
- A crime
- A question to be answered
- An investigation
- Suspense and climax

Realistic Fiction
- Stories that could happen
- Imaginary families
- Stories that help us learn about ourselves

Science Fiction
- Possible future events
- Travel to other galaxies
- Stories about possible future inventions

Fairytales & Fantasy
- Dragons, wizards, imaginary characters and places
- Magic, heroes, villains
- Good vs. evil

Animals
- Talking animals
- Animals acting like people
- Imaginary stories about kids and their pets

Nonfiction

Adventure
- Exciting real journeys to interesting places
- Real explorers' journeys
- Real-life heroes

Historical Stories
- Stories about real life in other times
- True stories about real people from the past

Mystery
- A true crime
- True puzzles with no answers
- Unsolved mysteries about creatures like Bigfoot

Families
- Real-life families
- Stories of real people and real families
- Multicultural families

Science
- Scientific discoveries and inventions
- Information about our bodies
- The world and space

Biography
- True stories about real people
- Factual information about famous people
- Learning about others' lives

Nature
- The environment
- Taking care of the Earth
- Plant books
- Wildlife books

Interest Sheet

The interest sheet helps younger children think about things they like to do. An adult can then help translate their interests into possible reading topics.

Materials:
Page 134
Pencil/pen

Goals:
To determine your interests

To help select book topics which might interest you

Steps:
1. Fill out each of the boxes on the form.
2. Ask an adult to help you write book ideas.
3. Use this list to help you find your next book.

Just for Fun:
• Use a big piece of paper and answer the questions with drawings.
• Think of other things you really like.
• List your favorite books and look for other books like them.
• List your favorite computer programs.

Interest Sheet Example

1. Things I like to do at home

Color
Watch Movies
Play Barbies
Play Piano

Play Freeze tag
Play in my play
house

2. Things I really like to do at school

Play at recess
I like choosing time
Play with friends

3. My favorite movies, videos & T.V. shows

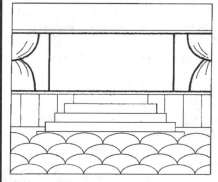 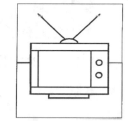

Flintstones

Hook, Aladdin
Beauty and the Beast
Wizard of Oz

Book Ideas

1. Animal books
   Musical books
   Picture books
2. Books about school
   " computers
   Family/friends
3. Fairy Tales
   Fantasy books
   Cartoon books
4. Basic-① How
   bodies work
   ② How cars
   work

4. Things I wonder about

Why do we grow bigger?
How do cars work?
How do we get our
voice?
How did we come
alive?

Our Favorite Books List

The students in Sue Parker's 6th–grade classroom, at Ben Rush Elementary School in Redmond, WA, conducted a schoolwide survey to create a list of each student's favorite book. This list (book and category) reflects each participating child's choice and perspective.

Materials:
Our favorite Book List
(pages 25–30)
Recommendation Form
(page 31)

Goal:
To select books using a book list recommended by other kids

Steps:
1. Find the genre (category) of book you like, such as picture books, sports, etc.
2. Find books that look interesting to you.
3. Write these on your "Books I Really Want to Read" Form (page 135)

Just for Fun:
- Do your own survey in your home, classroom, or school.
- Compare the books on this list to your favorite books.
- Select a book on the list randomly and read it to see how you like it.

Our Favorite Book List

(Students at Benjamin Rush Elementary School, Redmond, WA)

Adventure

Title	Author	Grade
The Littles	John Peterson	Second
Charlie and the Chocolate Factory	Roald Dahl	Third
James and the Giant Peach	Roald Dahl	
Farmer Boy	Laura Ingalls Wilder	Fourth
Watership Down	Richard Adams	
Where the Red Fern Grows	Wilson Rawls	
Hatchet	Gary Paulsen	Fifth
Island of the Blue Dolphins	Scott O'Dell	
Kara, The Lonely Falcon	Joseph Girzone	
The Call of the Wild	Jack London	
Where the Red Fern Grows	Wilson Rawls	
White Fang	Jack London	
Canyons	Gary Paulsen	Sixth
Cigars of the Pharaoh	Herge	
Hatchet	Gary Paulsen	
Homecoming	Cynthia Voigt	
Maniac Magee	Jerry Spinelli	
Mountain of Mirrors	Rose Estes	
On the Far Side of the Mountain	Jean Craighead George	
The Cay	Theodore Taylor	
The Time of the Witch	Mary Downing Hahn	
Tintin in Tibet	Herge	

Fiction

Title	Author	Grade
Henry and Mudge in the Sparkle Days	Cynthia Rylant	Second
Mister Popper's Penguins	Richard Atwater	
Oh, the Places You'll Go!	Dr. Seuss	
The Frog Prince, Continued	Jon Scieszka	
The Grouchy Ladybug	Eric Carle	
Tikki Tikki Tembo	Arlene Mosel	

Books Recommended by Kids

Fiction

Title	Author	Grade
Charlotte's Web	E.B. White	Third
Different Dragons	Jean Little	
Fourth Grade Rats	Jerry Spinelli	
Fudge-a-mania	Judy Blume	
Full House Same to You Duck	Bonnie Worth	
One Fat Summer	Robert Lipsyte	
Sarah, Plain and Tall	Patricia MacLachlan	
Socks	Beverly Cleary	
The Lion, the Witch and the Wardrobe	C.S. Lewis	
The Addams Family: A Novelization	Stephanie Calmenson	Fourth
The Legend of Huma	Richard A. Knaak	
The Wish Giver: Three Tales of the Coven Tree	Bill Brittain	
Mossflower	Brian Jacques	Fifth
Nothing's Fair in Fifth Grade	Barthe DeClements	
Sideways Stories from Wayside School	Louis Sacher	
The Sign of the Beaver	Elizabeth George Speare	
Where the Red Fern Grows	Wilson Rawls	
Dragonfire Volume 3	Morgana Rhys	Sixth
Prince Caspian	C.S. Lewis	
Winnie-the-Pooh	A.A. Milne	

Humor

Title	Author	Grade
Phil the Ventriloquist	Robert Kraus	Second
Esio Trot	Roald Dahl	Third
Matilda	Roald Dahl	
Beetles, Lightly Toasted	Phyllis Reynolds Nayler	Fourth
Esio Trot	Roald Dahl	
Full House Same to You Duck	Bonnie Worth	
Mrs. Piggle-Wiggle's Magic	Betty MacDonald	
Nothing's Fair in Fifth Grade	Barthe DeClements	
The Fourth Grade Wizards	Barthe DeClements	
There's a Boy in the Girls' Bathroom	Louis Sacher	

Humor

Title	Author	Grade
BFG	Roald Dahl	Fifth
Hank the Cowdog	John R. Erickson	
Matilda	Roald Dahl	
There's a Boy in the Girls' Bathroom	Louis Sacher	
Alice in Rapture, Sort Of	Phyllis Reynolds Naylor	Sixth
Merry Christmas, Amelia Bedelia	Peggy Parlsh	
Santa Cows	Cooper Edens	
Sideways Stories from Wayside School	Louis Sacher	
Sixth Grade Secrets	Louis Sacher	

Mystery

Title	Author	Grade
Werewolves Don't Go to Summer Camp	Debbie Dadey Marcia Jones	Second
Hardy Boys	Franklin Dixon	Third
Egypt Game	Zilpha Keatly Snyder	Fourth
Fear Street Series	R. L. Stine	
Great Christmas Kidnapping Caper	Jean Van Leeuwen	
Fear Street Series	R. L. Stine	
Mystery of the 99 Steps	Carolyn Keene	
Nate the Great	Marjorie Sharmat	
River Heights #1: Love Times Three	Carolyn Keene	
The Boxcar Children #20	Gertrude Chandler Warner	
The Chessmen of Doom	John Bellairs	
The Dead Man in Indian Creek	Mary Downing Hahn	
The Letter, the Witch, and the Ring	John Bellairs	
Bones on Black Spruce Mountain	David Budbill	Fifth
Bury Me Deep	Christopher Pike	
Mystery of the 99 Steps	Carolyn Keene	
Spellbound	Christopher Pike	
Stay Out of the Basement	R. L. Stine	
The Doll in the Garden	Mary Downing Hahn	
The True Confessions of Charlotte Doyle	Avi	
To Grandmother's House We Go	Willo Davis Roberts	

Mystery

Title	Author	Grade
Beach House	R. L. Stine	Sixth
Dead on Target (Hardy Boys Casefiles #1)	Franklin Dixon	
Elizabeth Gail and the Mystery at the Johnson Farm	Hilda Stahl	
Ski Weekend: Fear Street Series	R.L. Stine	
Something Upstairs	Avi	
The Baby-sitter	R.L. Stine	
The Knife: Fear Street Series	R.L. Stine	
The Mystery of the Fire Dragon	Carolyn Keene	
The Overnight: Fear Street Series	R.L. Stine	
The Westing Game	Ellen Raskin	
What Could Go Wrong	Willow Davis Roberts	
Vampire Vacation	Thomas McKean	

Nonfiction

Title	Author	Grade
Animal Families	Marilyn Mangus	Second
Fire Fighters	Robert Maas	
Kings of Creation	Don Lessem	
Nine True Dolphin Stories	Margaret Davidson	
Rain Forest Secrets	Arthur Dorros	
Reptile	Colin McCarthy, Nick Arnold	
How Long, Great Pumpkin, How Long	Charles M. Schulz	Third
Mysteries of Outer Space	Franklyn Branley	
Abraham Lincoln: The Great Emancipator	Augusta Stevenson	Fourth
Helen Keller	Margaret Davidson	
Lincoln: A Photobiography	Russell Freedman	Fifth

Picture Books

Title	Author	Grade
A Porcupine Named Fluffy	Helen Lester	Second
Bailey Goes Camping	Kevin Henkes	

Picture Books

Title	Author	Grade
Carl's Christmas	Alexandra Day	Second
Danny and the Dinosaur	Syd Hoff	
Fox in Socks	Dr. Seuss	
George's Marvelous Medicine	Roald Dahl	
I Just Forgot	Mercer Mayer	
If You Give a Mouse a Cookie	Laura Joffe Numeroff	
Imogene's Antlers	David Small	
Julius, the Baby of the World	Kevin Henkes	
Kites Sail High	Ruth Heller	
Little Grunt and the Big Egg	Tomie de Paola	
Mouse Soup	Arnold Lobel	
On Christmas Eve	Peter Collington	
Pecos Bill: A Tall Tale	Steven Kellogg	
Pinkerton, Behave!	Steven Kellogg	
Prince William	Gloria Rand	
Sylvester and the Magic Pebble	William Steig	
The Talking Eggs	Robert D. San Souci	
The Tale of the Mandarin Ducks	Katherine Paterson	
The Ballad of Mr. Tubbs	Pierre Houde	
The Cake that Mack Ate	Rose Robart	
Tigress	Helen Cowcher	
Willy the Wimp	Anthony Browne	

Poetry

Title	Author	Grade
A Light in the Attic	Shel Silverstein	Second
The Giving Tree	Shel Silverstein	
The New Kid on the Block	Jack Prelutsky	
Where the Sidewalk Ends	Shel Silverstein	

Realistic Fiction

Title	Author	Grade
Changes for Samantha: A Winter Story	Valerie Tripp	Second
Samantha Books	Valerie Tripp	
The Magic School Bus on the Ocean Floor	Joanna Cole	

Realistic Fiction

Title	Author	Grade
Socks	Beverly Cleary	Third
Anne of Green Gables	L.M. Montgomery	Fourth
On the Banks of Plum Creek	Laura Ingalls Wilder	
Five Finger Discount	Barthe DeClements	Fifth
Gone with the Wind	Margaret Mitchell	
Little House on the Prairie	Laura Ingalls Wilder	
My Side of the Mountain	Jean Craighead George	
Naya Nuki: Girl Who Ran	Kenneth Thomasma	
Up Periscope	Robb White	
A Little Princess	Frances Hodgson Burnett	Sixth
Alice in Rapture, Sort of	Phyllis Reynolds Naylor	
Avalanche!	An Rutgers Van der Loeff	
Forever	Judy Blume	
Island of the Blue Dolphins	Scott O'Dell	
Little Women	Louisa May Alcott	
Maniac Magee	Jerry Spinelli	

Sports

Title	Author	Grade
Long Shot for Paul	Matt Christopher	Fourth
Tough to Tackle	Matt Christopher	
Magic/Earvin "Magic" Johnson and Richard Levin	Earvin Johnson and Rich Levin	Sixth

Books We Recommend

Title	Author

Reading Idea List

The idea list helps readers select their next book from a list of books they really want to read. This list can be added to as they learn about new books from book-talks (page 76) or book-sells (page 74).

Materials:
Page 135
Book list (pages 25–31)
Pencil/pen

Goals:
To determine titles for future reading
To continue listing new book ideas

Steps:
1. List the books you want to read.
2. Keep your list handy so you can write new book ideas as you think of them.
3. Check off the book title and record the date when you've finished reading your book.

Just for Fun:
• Write down book ideas as you listen to book-talks or book-sells by others at school.
• Trade book recommendations with friends and see how you like their choices.

Reading Idea List Example

Name: Kaili

Books I Really Want To Read !

Title	Author	Genre	I read it! ✓
Marial of Redwall	Brian Jacques	Fiction	
The Cay	Theodore Taylor	Adventure	✓
Call of the Wild	Jack London	Adventure	
Sign of the Beaver	Elizabeth George Spear	Fiction	✓
Sixth Grade Secrets	Louis Sacher	Humor	

Reading Record

This log can be kept separately or in a folder with the Response Journal (page 55). You might also try recording pages read each day in a reading calendar.

Materials:
Page 136
Pencil/pen/markers

Goal:
To record the pages you read at each sitting

Steps:
1. Write today's date.
2. Write the name of the book you are reading.
3. Write the page number where you stopped reading.
4. Draw a symbol you design under "page" on the form when you have finished reading your book.

Just for Fun:
• Place a special sticker under "page" when you have finished your book.
• Create your own reading record folder.
• Keep a reading record at home and school.

Reading Record Example

My Reading Record

Name: Philip

Date	Book Title	Page
1-11	Henry and Ribsy	39-45
1-13	"	45-53
1-15	"	53-70

Genre Sampling

This is a fun way to sample the many types of books available to readers. Students enjoy brainstorming other genre toppings for the pizza like poetry. Lori Blevins Gonwick's 3rd-grade students love her genre pizzas.

Materials:
Page 137
Pencil
Large Paper Pizza Shape

Goal:
To read many types (genres) of books

Steps:
1. Choose the genre you want to try first.
2. Find a book in this genre and read it.
3. When you've finished reading your book, write the title and author in the topping.
4. When you have read each of the types of books, celebrate with a pizza.

Just for Fun:
Create your own personal paper genre pizza for your desk.

Genre Sampling Example

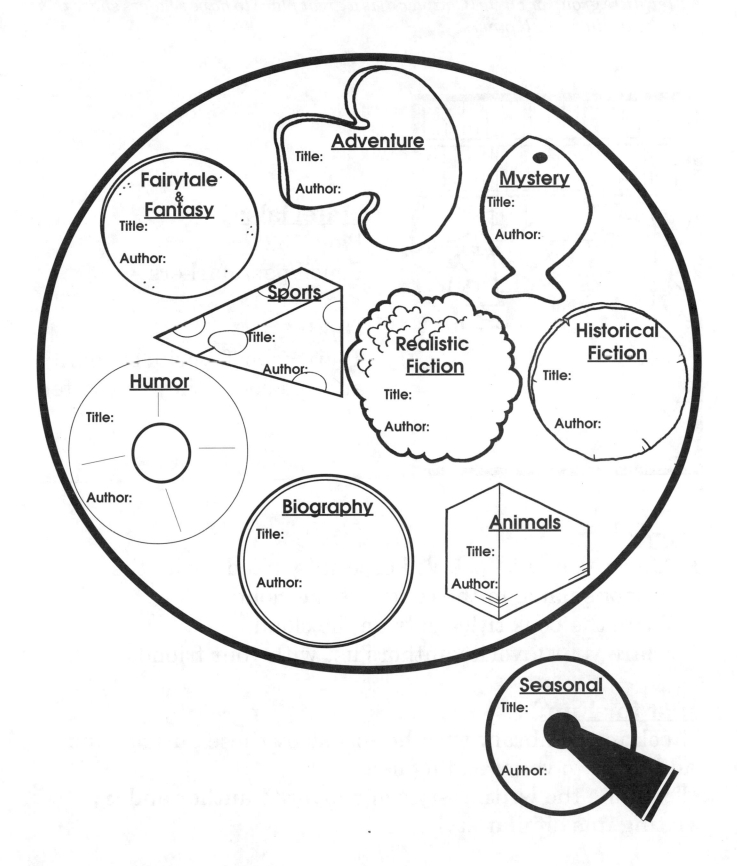

Adventure
Title:
Author:

Fairytale & Fantasy
Title:
Author:

Mystery
Title:
Author:

Sports
Title:
Author:

Realistic Fiction
Title:
Author:

Historical Fiction
Title:
Author:

Humor
Title:
Author:

Biography
Title:
Author:

Animals
Title:
Author:

Seasonal
Title:
Author:

Thanks to Robby Ricker (3rd-grade) for pizza cutter idea

Favorite Authors Sheet

A literature group or circle (Chapter 5) is a great place to have readers share their favorite authors with others.

Materials:
Page 138
Pencil/pen/markers

Goal:
To list your favorite authors
and the books they've written

Steps:
1. After reading a book you especially liked, write the author's name in the center of one cloud.
2. Write the book titles outside the cloud.
3. Share your favorite authors list with your friends.

Just for Fun:
• Look in the library for other books by these authors and add them to your reading list.
• Examine the writing style of a favorite author and try writing in a similar style.

Favorite Authors Sheet Example

Name: Erin

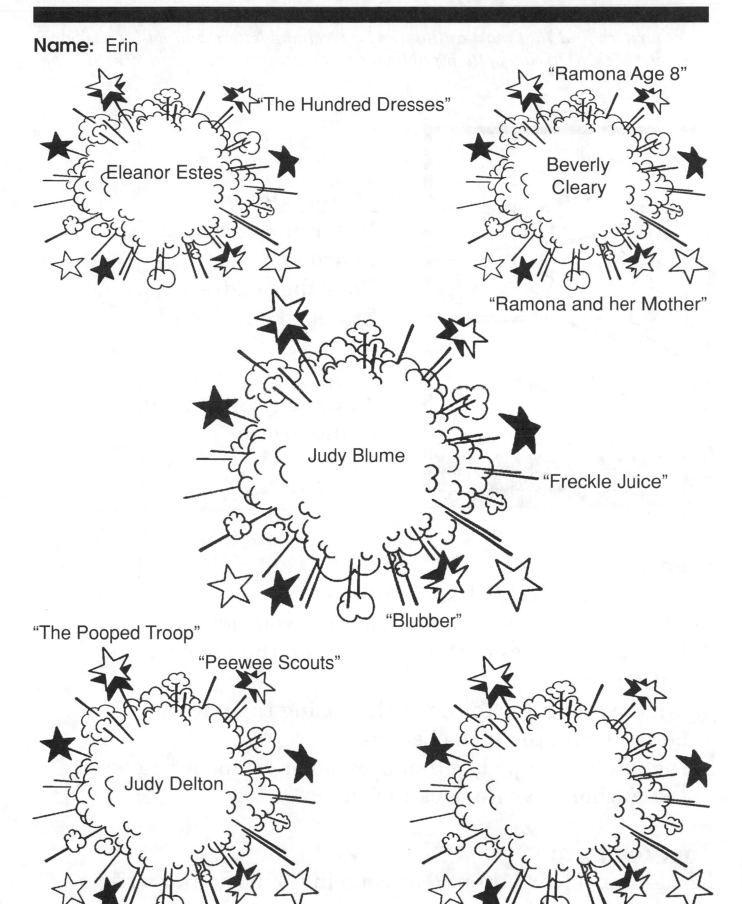

"The Hundred Dresses"

"Ramona Age 8"

Eleanor Estes

Beverly Cleary

"Ramona and her Mother"

Judy Blume

"Freckle Juice"

"Blubber"

"The Pooped Troop"

"Peewee Scouts"

Judy Delton

Letter to an Author

Letter writers find that most authors enjoy receiving letters and will write back if the letter is sent in care of their publisher and there is a return address from the writer.

Materials:
Paper and checklist
Pencil/pen
Publisher address
Stamped envelope

Goal:
To write a letter to an author or illustrator

Steps:
1. Look at the Letter Idea Checklist.
2. Check what you want to include in your letter.
3. Find the address of the publisher on the inside of the author's book.
4. Write your letter to the author using the publisher's address and the idea checklist.
5. Include a stamped, self-addressed envelope if you want the author to write back to you.

Just for Fun:
Design a postcard around a scene in the book and write a letter on it.

Letter to an Author Example

Mr. Louis Sacher
Avon Books
1350 Ave. of the Americas
New York, NY 10019

Dear Mr. Sacher,

Hi! My name is Brian Schnierer. I am going to be 9. I live in Woodinville, Washington. These are a couple of questions I would like you to answer please.

Where do you live? What's your favorite thing to do? When was the first book you made? How old were you when you made your first book? Are you married? How much children do you have? What is your favorite book that you made? Who is your favorite author besides you? Who is your favorite illustrator?

I put an envelope with my name and address inside so you can write me back. I really like your book Sideways Stories from the Wayside School. Why did you make Todd say he was stupid?

Please write me back. Thank you.

Brian S.

✓✓✓✓✓✓✓✓✓✓
Letter Idea Checklist

Things I want to include: ✍

Greeting (Hello, Hi)   ❑
Tell something about me   ❑
What I like in your book(s)   ❑
Tell why I am writing   ❑

Possible questions

Where do you live?   ○
Are you married?   ○
Do you have children?   ○
When did you write your first book?   ○
How old were you?   ○
Why do you write books?   ○
What do you like to write best?   ○
What are your writing strengths?   ○
What is hard for you to write?   ○
What is your favorite book?   ○
Who is your favorite author?   ○
Who is your favorite illustrator?   ○
Who is your favorite character in
   your books?   ○

Specific book questions   ❑
Closing (Thank you)   ❑
Sign my Name   ❑

Name:_____

Author Profile Sheet

It's fun for readers to learn about their favorite authors. This can be done by researching an author at the library, writing a letter to an author or by an interview with an author.

Materials:
Page 139
Pencil/pen

Goal:
To write biographical information about an author

Steps:
1. Go to the library to find out about an author or send a letter with the questions you want answered (see page 40).
2. Write the information you gather in the different folders and graphics.
3. Share your profile with friends who like the author too.

Just for Fun:
• Create your own form or use your own headings on a copy of this form.
• Interview an author in person.

Author Profile Example

Name: Jerry Yoo

(Michelle O'Brien-Palmer)

Michelle
38
Woodinvi'l,
Wa.

Author's name, age and home

The three books
The books are
Thorgh my eyes
Book write and
Book talk.

Number of books written and some book titles

Michelle
Nick
Gid
Sissy (cat)

Author's family

Poetry and how to write books.

Favorite type of writing

becquse it is crative and fun.

Why author likes to write

Illustrator Profile Example

Name: Brandon

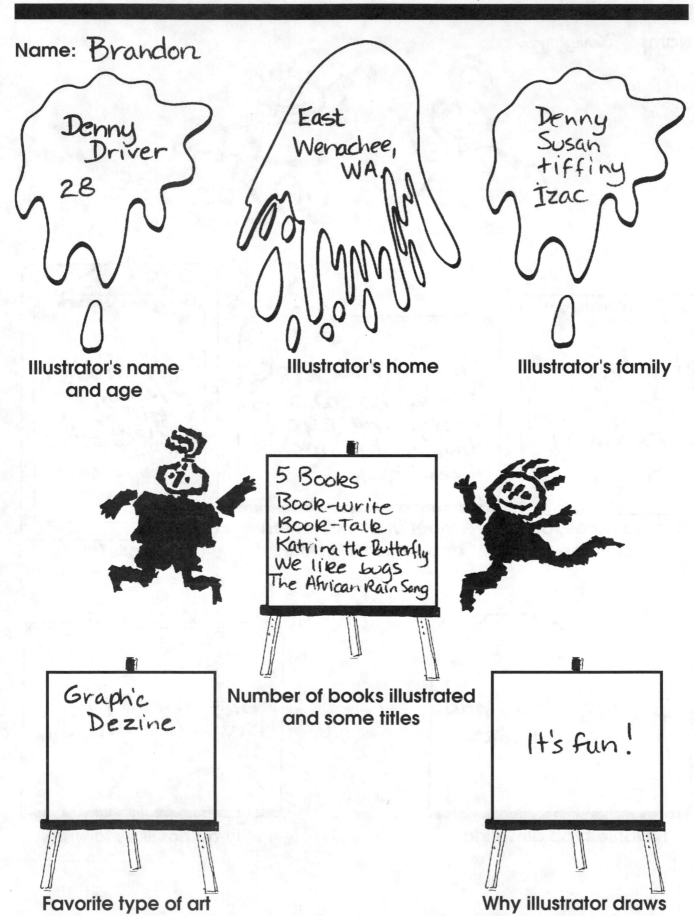

Denny Driver 28

Illustrator's name and age

East Wenachee, WA.

Illustrator's home

Denny Susan tiffiny Izac

Illustrator's family

5 Books
Book-write
Book-Talk
Katrina the Butterfly
We like bugs
The African Rain Song

Number of books illustrated and some titles

Graphic Dezine

Favorite type of art

It's fun!

Why illustrator draws

Illustrators Example

The Stories Julian Tells

Ann Strugnell

MORRIS HAS A COLD

Bernard Wiseman

Funny, Funny Lyle

Bernard Wader

Thanks to Molly Clark (6th-grade) for her rainbow idea

Chapter 3

Read and Respond

Read and Respond

"I love to read a good book because you just can't stop reading it and you always think about it." Sean Leverentz, 4th grade

Reading is an exciting personal adventure. Each person is touched by a book in a unique way. The experiences you've had in your life, your feelings about different things and what you know about the world influence how you respond to the book you are reading. One of the wonders of reading is a book's ability to pull you into its story. You can become a character; you can experience the book as if you were there.

This chapter presents many different ways to share your book experience with others.

"When I am reading it seems like I am part of the book."
Nick Palmer,
3rd grade

"Reading is like choosing your own adventure."
Sheetal Shah,
6th grade

"If when I'm reading I put my feelings inside the story, I know it's a good book!."

Michelle Kay,
3rd grade

"I love to read because while you are reading your book you feel like you're in a different world, and I enjoy being in those worlds."

Kristin Ware,
5th grade

About this Chapter

This chapter includes...

Story Sheet
Page 50
The story sheet helps younger readers respond to the story through three basic but thought-provoking questions. It helps them share their story experience.

Predictions
Page 52
Using a book cover, book title, or first paragraph, readers predict what they think might happen in a story. These predictions are based upon their life experience and knowledge. Predicting creates an incredible desire to read the story. Readers enjoy sharing and comparing their predictions.

Response Journal
Page 54
A journal allows the reader an opportunity to express his or her written response to the book. Response journals can take on many forms, both structured and unstructured. They vary from open-ended writing to the use of topic questions.

Story Maps
Page 56-59
Story maps help readers recognize and analyze the elements of a story. They provide a structure for talking about a story. This chapter shares three types of maps.

Retelling
Pages 60-65
Retelling stories through drawing, aloud, and writing, combines many literacy skills (reading, comprehension, thinking, remembering, organizing information, and communicating through writing). Retelling a story to others can be very empowering.

Comparisons
Pages 66-70
Readers are asked to identify similarities and differences between their predictions and the story as written by the author , between 2 or more stories, and between characters.

Story Sheet

The story sheet provides younger readers with a framework to discuss how they made meaning of a story.

Materials:
Page 142
Book
Pencil/Pen
Markers

Goal:
To think about things you noticed and felt when you read the story

Steps:
1. In the clouds, write things you noticed in the story.
2. Circle the faces that match the feelings you had when you read the story.
3. In the thunderbolts, write how the story reminds you of your life.

Just for Fun:
• Complete the story sheet after someone reads a story to you.
• Draw your own picture of the feelings you had as you read the story.

Story Sheet Example

Things I noticed in the story

(<u>The Foot Book</u> by Dr. Seuss)

Beginning   **Middle**   **End**

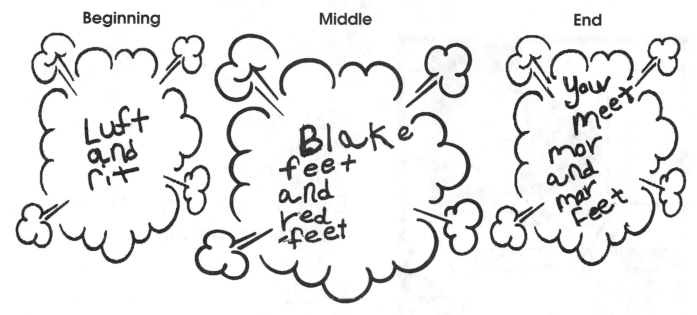

My Feelings

(Circle the feelings)

How this story reminds me of my life

Luft and rit Feet

Lechelle

it's a good Book

Predicting Story Outcomes

Predicting makes reading a book even more exciting. After predicting what we think might happen, we are eager to see how our predictions are similar to and different from what actually happens in the story.

Materials:
Paper
Pencil/Pen
Book of your choice
Computer (optional)

Goal:
To predict what will happen in a story

Steps:
1. Look at the cover, the title, or the first paragraph of the book you want to read.
2. Write your version of the story using the clues you find in the cover, title, or first paragraph (see examples).
3. Read the book to see how the author told the story.

Just for Fun:
• Draw your story prediction instead of writing it.
• Write a poem about what you think will happen in the book.

Story Outcome Prediction Examples

Prediction: Paragraph

Kaili Ka'lua'hini'nui Jackson

A Christmas Sonata
by Gary Paulsen

What I think is going to happen is that he overhears someone saying how all little kids believe in Santa Claus and how dumb it is.

The small boy hears that and is all sad that Santa Claus may not be real.

Prediction: Cover

It's the Soup that Made Me Sad
by Shannon Rubin

Steven Yoo

I think whats going to happen is that a girl went to a restrong and when they ordered some soup, the girl thought the bowl was small but when she looked at it, it looked big, its not big, it was huge.

Prediction: Book Title

Brian Schnierer

Chicken Sunday
by Patricia Polacco

One morning two kids took their mom and dad's cooking stuff out. They took the leftovers which were chicken, hot fudge and vanilla ice cream out of the re-fridgerator. They put it all in the mixer for two minutes. They poured it out in two glasses. One of the kids tried it and said "It's a miracle – it's delicious." The other kid tried it and said "you're right! It is delicious." So they went to a ice cream stand and sold it for $50.00 and they bought a nintendo game.

Response Journal

A response journal is a wonderful way to express the personal meaning a story has for you using the writing process. Journals can be private or shared. A journal can also be used in conjunction with the literature groups in Chapter 5.

Materials:
Paper
Pencil/Pen/Markers
Book

Goal:
To record your feelings and thoughts about the story you are reading

Steps:
1. Read in the book you've chosen.
2. Write or draw your thoughts and feelings about the story in your journal.
3. Share these with a friend or teacher.

Just for Fun:
• Make a special journal cover with inside pages.
• Use symbols from the stories you are reading to decorate your journal cover.

Response Journal Example

Phillip
January 15, 1993

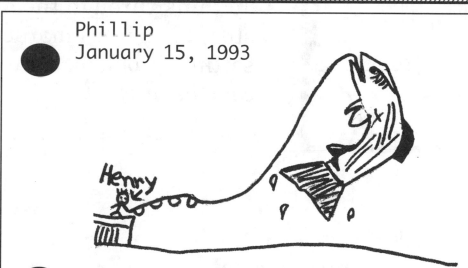

Henry's dad is thinking about takeing Henry fishing. I think Henry will catch a Chinhook. Henry has to keep his dog ribsy out of trouble inorder to go fishing. If I was Henry I would leash ribsy up. I feel that it is hard to keep your dog out of trouble.

This story taught me that if you have to do something give it your best shot.

Story Map

Story mapping helps readers recognize and analyze the elements of the story. A story map can take on many forms (see pages 57-59).

Materials:
Page 143
Paper
Pencil/Pen

Goal:
To think through the different story elements (characters, setting, problem, solution and conclusion)

Steps:
1. Read your book.
2. Think about each story element.
3. Fill in each box on the map.

Just for Fun:
• Design your own story map using circles or stars or some other shape.
• Create a group story map (see pages 58–59) on a white board or a piece of paper.

Story Map Individual Example

Name: Nick
Title: Helen Keller
Author: Margaret Davidson

CHARACTERS ▼

Helen Keller
Annie Sullivan
Mr. and Mrs. Keller

PROBLEM(S)▼

1. Helen got sick and she became blind, deaf and she couldn't talk.

2. Her parents didn't know what to do.

3. No one in her town knew how to communicate with her.

SETTING ▼

The story takes place in the late 1800's and early 1900's

In Alabama and Boston

SOLUTION(S)▼

Her parents called Annie Sullivan

She taught Helen how to talk

She taught her to read with her hands and communicate with her hands

She got her into the Perkins School for the Blind

Helen was able to ride horses

She went to college and she got to go to the White House and be in the paper

She became famous

CONCLUSION ▲

Group Story Map Example

Main Characters

Fern
Wilbur
Charlotte

Vocabulary

runt - small weakling
infant- baby
relieved-- to feel better
hullabaloo-
trough--
peered-- looked
vanished-- disappeared
slops--
and so on...

Supporting Characters

sheep	goose
teacher	pupils
Lurvy	rooster
Templeton	
Mr./Mrs. Zuckerman	
Mr./Mrs. Arables	

Charlotte's Web
by
E.B. White

Setting

Chapter 1: Morning time at Arables' Farm
Chapter 2: The Arables' Farm
Chapter 3: Zuckermans' Farm
and so on...

Chapter Title	Problem	Solution
1 Before Breakfast	Mr. Arable was planning to kill a runt piglet.	Fern stopped her dad and saved the piglet.
2 Wilbur	Wilbur is going to be sold by Mr. Arable	He gets sold to Fern's uncle, Mr. Zuckerman, so she can visit Wilbur.
and so on...		

Story map by Lori Blevins Gonwick's 3rd–grade classroom

Group Story Map Example

The Mitten
Jan Brett

Beginning:

Nick lost his mitten. First the mole found a nice cozy place in the mitten. Next the snowshoe rabbit squished in. Then they let the hedgehog in. Then the owl came in the mitten. Then the badger wiggled in too.

Climax:

The fox squished in and finally the bear scrunched in. The mouse got on the bear's nose and he sneezed.

Ending:

Nick found his mitten flying in the air like a bird.

Story map by Suzie Fiebig's 2nd-grade classroom

Retelling Through Drawing

Great fun for all ages but especially for non-writers. Retelling has been found to enhance students' reading/listening comprehension. The written description of the drawing example can be found on page 63.

Materials:
Paper
Pencil/pens
Markers/Crayons

Goal:
To retell a story through drawings

Steps:
1. Listen to a story or read a story yourself.
2. Draw one picture or a group of pictures that you will use to retell the story.
3. Share the pictures you've drawn with your friends.

Just for Fun:
• Draw pictures to express your <u>feelings</u> as you listened to the story.
• Paint a picture to illustrate a scene from the story as you listen.

Retelling Example

Goldilocks and the Three Bears, Retold by Lissa Rubin
(Written description on Page 63)

Retelling Aloud

It is very exciting for younger readers to respond to a story with artwork and then use their drawings to retell the story aloud in their own words. Having another person write down what they say is also very validating.

Materials:
Paper
Pencil/pens

Goals:
To retell a story
To remember the story
through your own drawings

Step:

1. Look at the story pictures you've drawn.
2. Tell what happens in each picture.
3. Listen as your friends share their drawings with the other students.

Just for Fun:

• Have someone write your story onto paper.
• Tape record the story as you retell it.
• Have someone videotape you as you retell the story.
• Tell your friend what you especially liked about his/her drawings.

Retelling Example

(Dictated by Lissa using her drawings on page 61.)

① Once upon a time there was a little cottage and there was 3 windows. There was really 4 but one of them went to the kitchen and there was 4 dots on each one cause that's how you pull the window parts out.

② Three bears lived in that place & and they went to get some honey. And there was a Papa Bear, Mama Bear and a Baby Bear. They went out to get some honey.

③ Then this little girl came. She saw the little cottage and then there was dark clouds. And so she had to get into the cottage really fast.

④ So she got into the cottage and found a table. She saw 3 bowls & 3 cups. She first tried the Papa Bear's cereal - it was too hot, then the Mama Bear's - it was too cold. Then she tried the Baby Bear's - it was just right.

⑤ Then she went upstairs & found 3 beds. She tried the Papa Bear's - it was too hard, the Mama Bear's was too soft. She tried the Baby Bear's bed and...

⑥ it was just right – so she went to sleep.

⑦ When the 3 bears came home...

⑧ they all went into their rooms and checked their beds. The Papa Bear said "Somebody was sleeping in my bed." The Mama Bear said "Somebody was sleeping in my bed." The Baby Bear said "and she's still there."

⑨ Goldilocks jumped out of bed & ran downstairs as fast as she could and she didn't know how to unlock it. She found that wood piece, picked it up, ran outside and peeked in the gate, shook it - it was locked.

⑩ And then there was a policeman and he opened the gate for her and he walked her to her house.

Retelling Through Writing

Retelling through writing combines many literacy skills: reading, comprehension, thinking, remembering, organizing information and communicating.

Materials:
Paper
Pencil/pen

Goal:
To retell a story
To share a favorite story with friends

Step:
1. Read your book.
2. Be sure that you really understand what you've read.
3. Without looking at the book, pretend you are writing the story down for a friend who hasn't read it, and that you want him to enjoy it as much as you did.
4. Write the story in your own words onto your paper.

Just for Fun:
Write a letter to a friend retelling the story.

Retelling Examples

Retelling
(2nd-grader: dictated)

Steven

It's the Soup that Made Me Sad by Shannon Rubin

Kimi's room was a mess and she couldn't find her baseball mitt so she couldn't play.

Then her dad called they're going out to dinner. When Kimi went out of her bed she tripped over the mitt and she said "stupid mitt."

Then they were at the restaurant and her mother said "what do you want for dinner" and she said "just soup." Then the soup came and when she looked at the soup it wasn't plain, it was big. It was huge. Everything in the soup made Kimi sad. She ate everything one by one.

Then she went to her room and picked stuff up one by one. And Kimi called her parents and told them that she cleaned up the mess.

Retelling
(3rd-grader)

Brian

Chicken Sunday

P.Polacco

A Grandmother named Miss Eula makes chicken dinner every Sunday and wants a special hat she can't buy. Her grandsons and the girl telling the story want to buy her that hat but they have to pay Mr. Kodinski. They don't have enough money so they paint eggs. Mr. Kodinski likes them and the kids sell them at his store. He gives them the pink hat for Miss Eula. She was real happy.

Retelling
(6th-grader)

Name: Kaili
Book Title: A Christmas Sonata
Book Author: Gary Paulson

The story is about a boy who see's a neighbor in a Santa outfit and thinks that there isn't a real Santa.

He gets really sad and is mad at his mom and dad. He thinks that there is no real meaning to Christmas. Then when he is with his dying cousin on Christmas Eve night the small boys Uncle Ben is reading a story when he says he heard bells. They run outside and they see four real reindeer and one real Santa. The small boys believed in him from then on.

Prediction Comparisons

Once a story has been retold, the reader can then analyze the similarities and differences between her prediction and the story as written by the author.

Materials:
Prediction sheet
Retelling sheet
Paper
Pencil/pens

Goal:
To compare your prediction with the story as written by the author

Steps:

1. Reread your completed book prediction and your retelling of the story.
2. Using the questions below or the comparison forms on page 144–145, identify the similarities and differences between your prediction and retelling.

Just for Fun:
Write your own story using your prediction to guide you.

Possible Comparison Questions
How did your prediction match the story? What clues led to your prediction? Which story do you like best? How would you change the story?

Comparison Examples

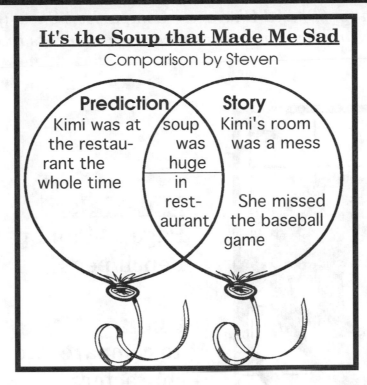

It's the Soup that Made Me Sad
Comparison by Steven

Prediction
Kimi was at the restaurant the whole time

soup was huge in restaurant

Story
Kimi's room was a mess

She missed the baseball game

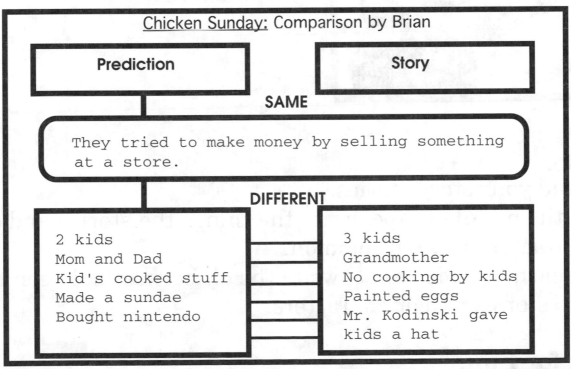

Chicken Sunday: Comparison by Brian

Prediction

Story

SAME

They tried to make money by selling something at a store.

DIFFERENT

2 kids
Mom and Dad
Kid's cooked stuff
Made a sundae
Bought nintendo

3 kids
Grandmother
No cooking by kids
Painted eggs
Mr. Kodinski gave kids a hat

Prediction	**A Christmas Sonata**	**Story**
Small boy overhears someone say that there was no Santa. He's really sad	Comparison by Kaili The small boy thinks that Santa isn't real.	He saw a fake Santa drinking wine. He learned the true meaning of Christmas through his cousin.

Comparison Sheets

The Venn Diagram (p. 69) and Character Comparison Sheet (p.70) both provide the opportunity to compare and contrast various elements in a story.

Materials:
Page 144 and page 145
Pencil/pens

Goal:
To compare two stories or characters

Steps:
1. Read your story/stories.
2. In the middle shape, write the things the stories and/or characters have in common.
3. In each outside shape, write the differences between the two stories and/or characters.

Just for Fun:
- Create a Venn using two balloons (see page 67).
- Try comparing two books, a movie and book, two characters or two versions of the same story.

Venn Diagram Example

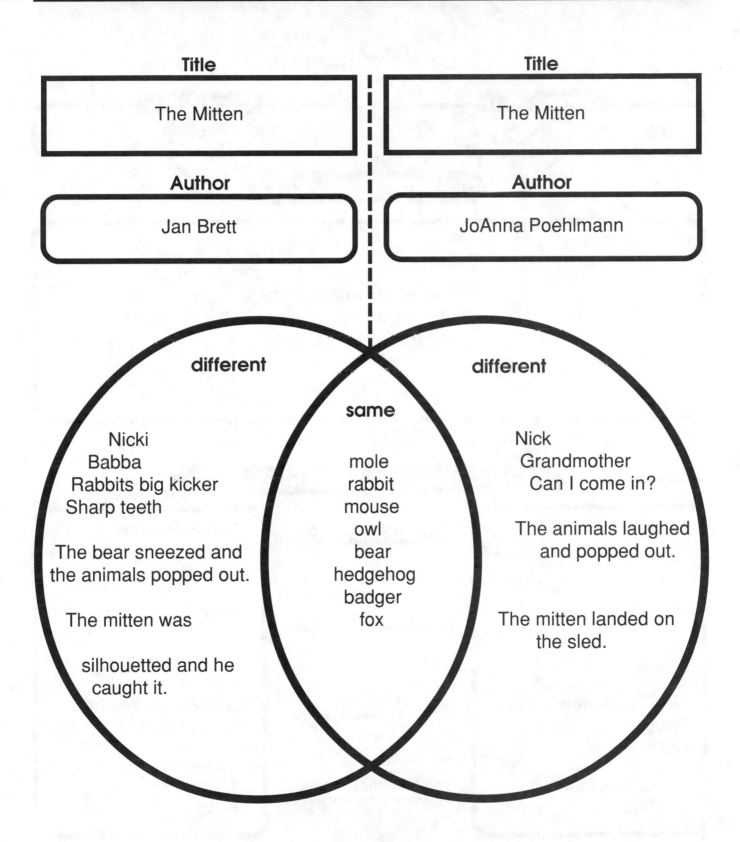

Title

The Mitten

Title

The Mitten

Author

Jan Brett

Author

JoAnna Poehlmann

different

Nicki
Babba
Rabbits big kicker
Sharp teeth

The bear sneezed and
the animals popped out.

The mitten was

silhouetted and he
caught it.

same

mole
rabbit
mouse
owl
bear
hedgehog
badger
fox

different

Nick
Grandmother
Can I come in?

The animals laughed
and popped out.

The mitten landed on
the sled.

Suzie Fiebig's 2nd-grade classroom

Character Comparison Example

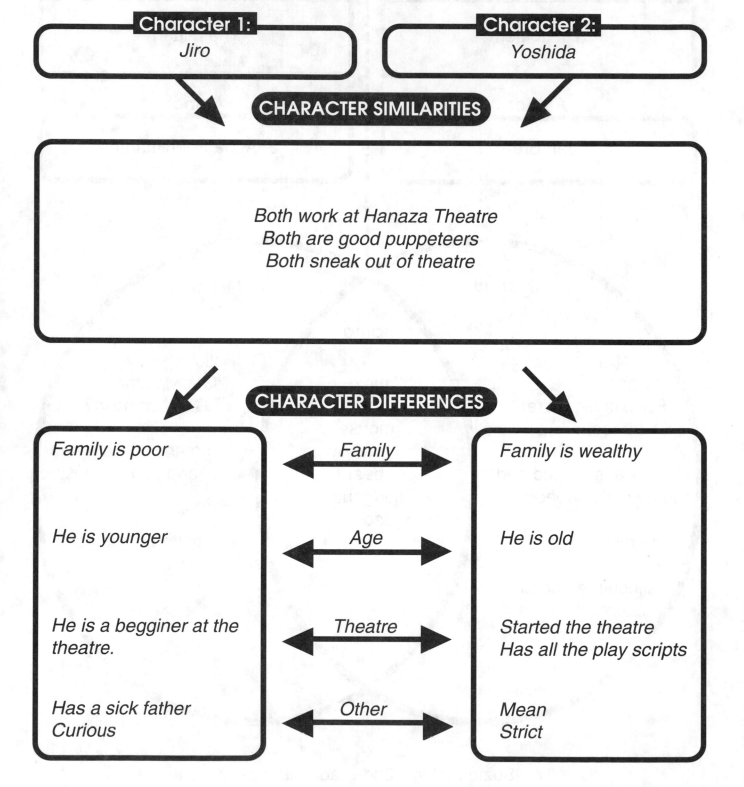

The Master Puppeteer

Character 1:
Jiro

Character 2:
Yoshida

CHARACTER SIMILARITIES

Both work at Hanaza Theatre
Both are good puppeteers
Both sneak out of theatre

CHARACTER DIFFERENCES

Family is poor	Family	Family is wealthy
He is younger	Age	He is old
He is a begginer at the theatre.	Theatre	Started the theatre Has all the play scripts
Has a sick father Curious	Other	Mean Strict

by Juleah Swanson

Chapter 4

Read and Review

Read and Review

"A good book is a book I like to read because it's fun to read and exciting." Ed Lobdell, 1st grade

As we read a book, we evaluate (judge) it many times. If it captures our interest we are drawn into the story. Many people have difficulty putting a great book down. If it doesn't capture our attention we may lose interest and put it aside. If the story doesn't make sense to us or we don't understand what is going on, we feel frustrated.

There are many ways to review a book. As with reading, reviewing a book is very personal. We each evaluate a book through our own interests and personal experience of it. Reviewing a book means determining what you thought of the book, how you liked it, how much of a challenge it was to you, and whether or not you would recommend it to a friend.

Book reviews can be written or given orally (out loud). Book-Sells (p.74) and Book-Talks (p.76) are usually oral. Pizza Reports (p. 86) and Remarkable Reviewer Reviews (p. 83-85) are written.

When you review a book, you share your reading experience with others. **Your opinion is very important and may help others in selecting their next books.**

"I like books to have a happy ending and a good starting and things that I like in them."

Tiffany Driver, 2nd grade

"I think a book's really good when the author puts excitement into the book and shows a character's talent ."

Gavin Schroder, 4th grade

"A good book is one that interests you, that keeps your attention and makes you want to read on."

Emily Mack, 5th grade

About This Chapter

This chapter includes...

Oral Book Reviews

Book-Sell
Page 74
Readers take a book they really like and "sell" it to their friends in a book-sell. Kids love to do their book-sell while being video-taped (like on the TV show "Reading Rainbow").

Book-Talk
Page 76
A more in-depth review of a book than in the book-sell. The Book-Talk Checklist helps presenters to determine the content of their talk and think through their presentation style.

Oral Review Evaluations

Self Evaluations

Book-Sell
Page 78
open-ended questions which help a presenter think through his or her book-sell

Book-Talk
Page 79
rating scale with an action plan

Buddy Evaluations

Book-Sell
Page 80
introduction to thinking through another person's presentation

Book-Talk
Page 81
open-ended questions and rating scale to give feedback

Written Book Reviews

Remarkable Reviewer
Pages 83-85   three review formats: this book's hot, not hot, or OK!

Pizza Reports
Page 86   introduction to book evaluation using pizza topping shapes

Bubble Gum Review
Page 88   Write or draw your review in gumballs.

Giving Book-Sells

Kids love to do book-sells. They are eager to do them after watching the public television show "Reading Rainbow." See pages 78 and 80 for the evaluation component.

Materials:
Paper/Pencil
Checklist
Book
Video camera
Reading Rainbow TV Show

Goal:
To persuade others to read your book

Steps:
1. Watch several "Reading Rainbow" TV shows (check local listings for time).
2. Note some book-sell ideas from "Reading Rainbow" kids (your favorite slogans etc.)
3. Use the checklist (page 75) to be sure that you include all the information you want to include in your book-sell.
4. Write your book-sell draft.
5. Practice with a friend and make revisions.
6. Have someone videotape your book-sell.

Just for Fun:
Break into pairs and do a book-sell together.

Book-Sell Examples

A Book-Sell Checklist

- ❏ Your Name
- ❏ Book Title, Author, Illustrator
- ❏ Genre (type of book)
- ❏ Character(s)
- ❏ Problem(s)
- ❏ How you feel about this book
- ❏ Something interesting about the story (but don't give the ending away!)
- ❏ Invite the audience to READ THIS BOOK!

Nick

Book-Sell

Hi! My name is Nick. I just read a great book called "Helen Keller." It's a true story.

Can you imagine what it would be like to always be in the dark and never hear a sound? Can you imagine not communicating with other people? Well, that's what Helen Keller's life was like.

Find out how Helen was helped by her friend Annie and became famous. Read this great book!

Steven

Book-Sell

Hi! My name is Steven Yoo. I just read "It's the Soup That Made Me Sad." I really liked it.

Kimi has a problem. Her room is a mess and she can't find her baseball mitt. So she can't go to the game with her friends.

To see how a huge bowl of soup helps Kimi to clean up her room, you've got to read this book!

Book-Talk

A book-talk is usually given by more experienced readers. When preparing for a book-talk, it helps to look at presentation content and style separately (see page 77). Thanks to Sue Parker (6th-grade teacher) for her evaluation ideas.

Materials:
Checklists on page 77
Paper/Pencil
Book

Goal:
To share the book you've read with others

Steps:
1. Think about what you find interesting in the book-talks you've seen and write it down.
2. List what makes a speaker's style interesting to you.
3. Use the Book-Talk Content Checklist (page 77) to select the items you want to include in your book-talk.
4. Write a draft of your book-talk.
5. Reread your style notes and style checklist (page 77).
6. Practice with a friend and revise.
7. Give your book-talk.

Just for Fun:
Write your book-talk out on colored index cards.

Book-Talk Content Checklist

My Book-Talk

The *Master Puppeteer* is an awsome book. It was written by Katherine Paterson who has won two Newberry Awards. The illustrator, Haru Wells animated some cartoons for Sesame Street. I chose the book because it's a Newberry Award winner and it takes place in Japan with a Japanisse heritage. I like this book because it is a mixture book. It is sad, happy, part mystery, and very good. The book could also be the Japinisse version of Robin Hood because a mysterious man steals from the rich and gives to the poor or hungry. Jiro, the main character, wants to know who the mysterious man (Saburo) is. Saburo has appeared at many places, even Hanza Puppet Theatre, but no one has ever seen him.

I learned about puppeteering in Japan. Puppeteering sounds fun and hard. I would like to try it some day. I think the author wrote it because it is such an interesting subject. Some changes I would make are making Saburo come up more in the beginning, and make it more a mystery.

Other books by Katherine Paterson are *Bridge to Terrbithia*, and *The Sign of the Chrysanthe*. I hope you read the master puppeteer and enjoy it as much as I did.

by Juleah

Name:

Book-Talk Content Checklist

Things I want to include in my book-talk:

1
- ☐ Book Title, Author, Illustrator
- ☐ Genre
- ☐ Visual about the book (see Chapter)
- ☐ My challenge level low 1•2•3•4•5 high
- ☐ Catchy opening statement
  (tell something interesting)

2
- ☐ What attracted me to the book
- ☐ Short problem summary
- ☐ What I liked/didn't like
- ☐ Overall rating 1-10
- ☐ The changes I'd make to the story

3
- ☐ Other books by this author
- ☐ Information about the author
- ☐ Information about the illustrator
- ☐ Snappy closing summary
- ☐ Would I recommend this book? (Why?)

Book-Talk Style Checklist

- ☐ **Eye Contact**
  Look at your audience

- ☐ **Voice**
  Speak slowly, clearly

- ☐ **Voice**
  Speak loudly enough

- ☐ **Enthusiasm**
  High energy level

Book-Sell Self-Evaluation Form

Name:
Book Title:
Book Author:

My Book-Sell

1. How did you like doing your book-sell? Please explain.

2. How did you feel watching your book-sell videotape?
   Please give details.

3. Do you think your book-sell was interesting? Yes ❑   No ❑
   What was the most interesting part of your book-sell?

4. If you could change something about your book-sell, what
   would it be?

Book-Talk Self-Evaluation Form

My Book-Talk Self-Evaluation

Book Title:

Book Author:

My Rating Scale
Need practice   Met my goal
1•2•3•4•5

CONTENT

Was I interesting? --- 1•2•3•4•5
Did my opening catch my audience's attention? ---- 1•2•3•4•5
Did I pique my audience's interest? ----------------------- 1•2•3•4•5
Did I tell too much about the story? ----------------------- 1•2•3•4•5
Did I have a good closing statement? -------------------- 1•2•3•4•5
Did I mention other books by this author? ---------------- 1•2•3•4•5

STYLE

Did I make eye contact with my audience? ------------- 1•2•3•4•5
How was my voice quality? ---------------------------------- 1•2•3•4•5
Was my visual presentation bright and colorful? ------ 1•2•3•4•5
Did I show enthusiasm for my book? ---------------------- 1•2•3•4•5

The part I liked best about my book-talk was:

In my next book-talk, the one thing I am going to do differently will be:

Signed_____

Book-Sell Buddy Review Form

Book-Sell Buddy Review

Date:
Presenter's Name: _____
Book Title:_____

1. Do you want to read this book now? Yes ☐ No ☐
   Why?

2. What was your favorite part of the book-sell?
   Please explain.

3. What do you think was the most interesting part of
   the book-sell?

Signed _____

Beyond Book Reports Scholastic Inc.

Book-Talk Buddy Review Form

Book-Talk Buddy Review

Date:
Name of Presenter:
Name of Book:

Rating Scale
Needs practice — Great job

Content

Kept my interest -----------------	1•2•3•4•5
Catchy opening -----------------	1•2•3•4•5
Story information ---------------	1•2•3•4•5
Author information -------------	1•2•3•4•5
Closing summary ---------------	1•2•3•4•5

Style

Eye contact ---------------------	1•2•3•4•5
Voice quality -------------------	1•2•3•4•5
Visual presentation quality -----	1•2•3•4•5
Book enthusiasm ---------------	1•2•3•4•5

After hearing this book-talk ❏ I am/❏ I am not interested in reading this book. I based this opinion on:

The things I really liked in your book-talk:

Ideas for future book-talks:

Signed _____

Remarkable Reviewer Reviews

The Remarkable Reviewer sheets can be used once a reader is familiar with story elements. A book will fall into one of three categories: hot, not hot, or OK. This helps categorize books for others who may be interested in a certain title.

Materials:
Pages 146-148
Paper
Pencil/Pen

Goals:
To review a book
To share your review with others

Steps:
1. Read your book.
2. Decide which category you think this book fits into: Hot, Not Hot, or OK.
3. Answer the questions on the sheet you've chosen.
4. Share your review with friends.

Just for Fun:
•Design your own review form(s).
•Create notebooks for each category.
•Color code each type of review.
•Place reviews into three different colored file folders.

Remarkable Reviewer

This Book's HOT!

My Challenge Scale
Low 1 • 2 • ③ • 4 • 5 High

Name: _Shannon Bovan_

Title
The Stories Julian Tells

Author
Ann Cameron

Illustrator
Ann Strugnell

Characters
Julian
Gloria

Setting
Not sure

Summary

The dad spends like an hour making pudding for the mom and used like twenty lemons and a dozen and a half eggs. And the kids eat it all and hid under the bed. The dad comes in and sees the goop on the floor.

I chose this book because:
I liked the names of the stories. One was eating lemon pudding their dad was making for their mom's birthday.

My favorite part of this book was:
When the kids get in trouble from their dad for eating their mom's pudding and they hid under the bed.

Remarkable Reviewer

This Book's NOT HOT!

My Challenge Scale
Low 1 • 2 • 3 • 4 • 5 High

Name: Kaili

Title
Where the Red Fern Grows

Author
Wilson Rawls

Illustrator

Characters
Julian
Gloria

Setting
Hunting
House

Summary

A boy gets two puppies that are hunting dogs. He takes them out for hunting. One got killed in the beginning of hunting and the next got killed too. The dogs were buried at his house. When he had to move he didn't want to because his dogs were still there. Then a red fern grows in between the place where the two dogs are buried. It is an Indian symbol and then he felt better about moving.

I chose this book because:
Someone said it was a good book.

I didn't like this book because:
It was really gross and sad. One part: the boy falls on an axe and the author discribes it very clearly. The boy has blood bubles coming out of his mouth (that is just one of the gross seens.) Then the dogs (2 dogs) die and the author discribes that very clearly. I also hate any book that has a pet dieing.

Remarkable Reviewer

This Book's <u>OK</u>

My Challenge Scale
Low 1•2•3•4•5 High

Name: Terry Yoo

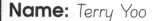

Title
Harriet Tubman

Author
Kate McMullan

Illustrator
· Steven James

Characters
Harriet Tubman   John Tubman
Harriet's friends   Slaves

Summary

Sometimes she is a slave. She rescued over 300 slaves. She got something from Queen Victoria. Harriet Tubman is a famous person. She got into a lot of adventures.

Setting

At her house

I chose this book because:
It was a famous person book.

The reason I think this book is just OK is:
I like books about boys better.

I would recommend it to a friend: YES ☑ NO ☐

Please explain: I think it is a good book but not my favorite kind of book.

Pizza Reports

This is a great evaluation tool for younger readers. Readers start with the Canadian bacon report for the first book, sausage for the next, and so on. By the fourth review, they have discussed setting, main characters, identified goals and summarized a plot.

Materials:
Pages 149-150
Pencil
Pizza bulletin board

Goals:
To write about story elements
To earn toppings to put on a pizza board

Steps:
1. Make a pizza shape for a bulletin board.
2. After reading your book, answer the questions in report 1. Use report 2 for the next book you read and so on.
3. Cut out the report topping and place it on the board.
4. Determine the number of toppings needed to complete the pizza.
5. When the board is filled with toppings, plan a pizza party to celebrate reading.

Just for Fun:
Make your own pizza topping shape reports.

Pizza Report Examples

Report 1: Setting Identification

Name:

Canadian Bacon Report

_____
Title of the book

Author_____

Illustrator_____

# of pages ___easy❑ medium❑ challenge❑

Where does the story take place?

_____

_____

_____

Do you recommend this book? Y N
Draw a picture of the setting
on the back

Report 2: Plot Identification

Name:

Sausage Report

Title _____

Author_____ Illustrator_____

# of pages___ easy ❑ medium❑ challenge❑

What happens at the beginning of the story?

What happens in the middle of the story?

What happens at the end of the story?

Do you like the ending?
Yes ❑ No ❑

Report 3: Story Summary

Name:

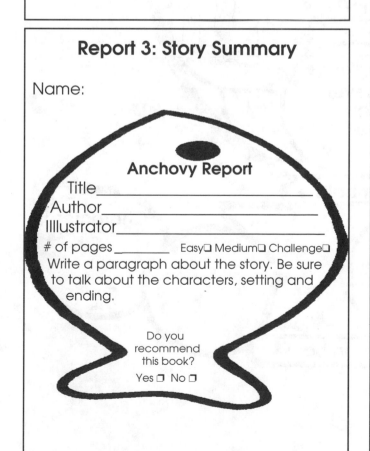

Anchovy Report

Title_____

Author_____

IIllustrator_____

# of pages_____ Easy❑ Medium❑ Challenge❑

Write a paragraph about the story. Be sure
to talk about the characters, setting and
ending.

Do you
recommend
this book?
Yes ❑ No ❑

Report 4: Main Character and Goal Identification

Name:

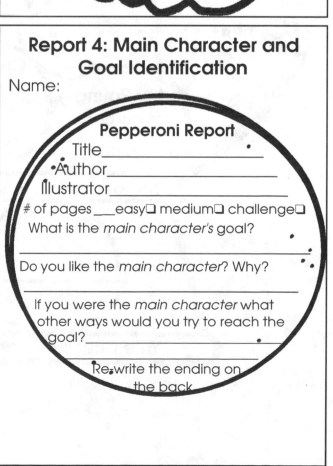

Pepperoni Report

Title_____

Author_____

Illustrator_____

# of pages ___easy❑ medium❑ challenge❑

What is the *main character's* goal?

_____

Do you like the *main character*? Why?

_____

If you were the *main character* what
other ways would you try to reach the
goal?_____

_____

Re-write the ending on
the back

Bubble Gum Review Example

Name: Nick

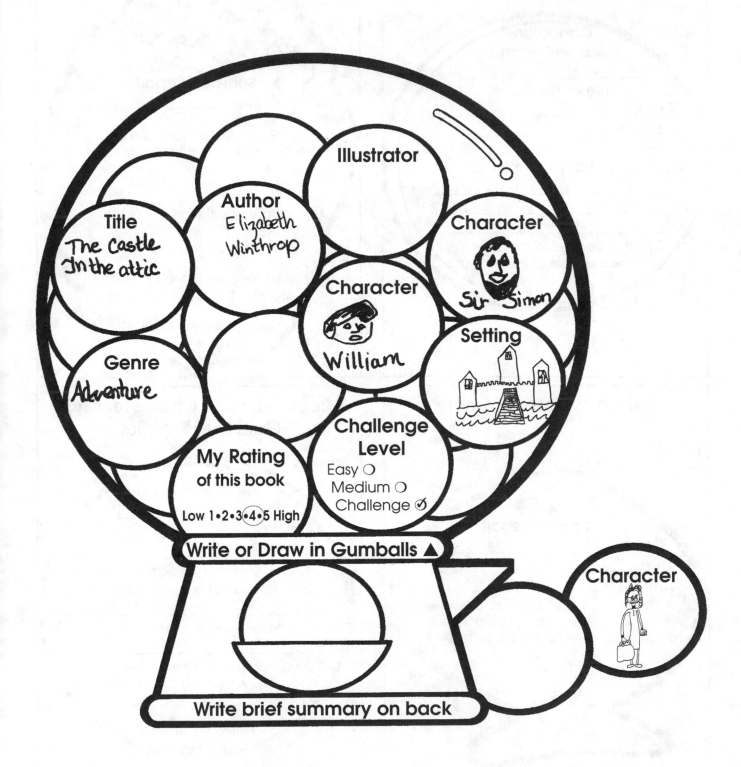

Illustrator

Author
Elizabeth
Winthrop

Title
The Castle
In the attic

Character
Sir Simon

Character
William

Genre
Adventure

Setting

My Rating
of this book

Low 1•2•3•4•5 High

Challenge
Level

Easy ○
Medium ○
Challenge ✓

Write or Draw in Gumballs ▲

Character

Write brief summary on back

Chapter 5

Literature Groups:
Getting Started

Literature Groups

"I like literature groups where we all talk about the same book."
Nick Palmer, 3rd grade

Sharing is a very enjoyable part of reading. This chapter is dedicated to sharing books in literature groups. Literature groups are sometimes called literature circles because the group takes place in a circle. There are usually five to seven members in a group. When a group first starts, it is helpful to have an adult leader get the group going. Later, many groups meet on their own.

Literature groups can share books in a variety of ways. This chapter provides starter questions for three ways to share books: books of the same genre, books by the same author, and story elements of the same book. However, the discussion possibilities are limitless as each unique literature group takes form.

This chapter also includes an evaluation component for literature group members and leaders.

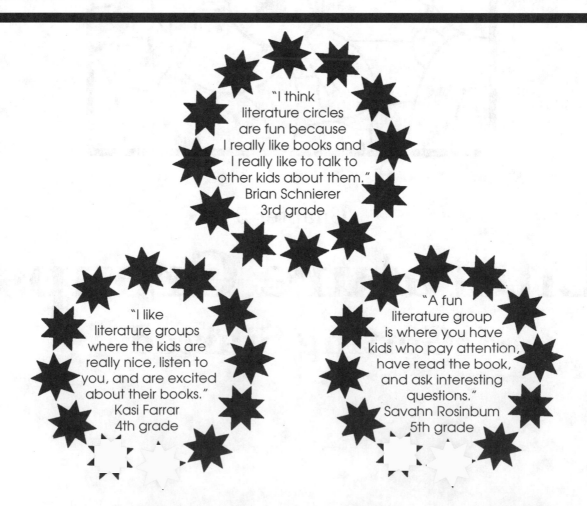

"I think literature circles are fun because I really like books and I really like to talk to other kids about them."
Brian Schnierer
3rd grade

"I like literature groups where the kids are really nice, listen to you, and are excited about their books."
Kasi Farrar
4th grade

"A fun literature group is where you have kids who pay attention, have read the book, and ask interesting questions."
Savahn Rosinbum
5th grade

About This Chapter

This chapter includes...

Book Selection
Two techniques for literature group book selection

Book Sharing
Page 92-93

Readers listen to a book share and fill out their own ballots.

Book Exchange
Page 94-95

Readers preview a number of books and record their notes.

Book Club Circle

Club Starters
Page 97

Provides four sessions of starter questions to get your book club going.

Literature Group Focus

Genre
Page 99

group starter questions for different types of books

Story Elements
Page 101

group starter questions for predicting story outcomes, setting development, character development, plot analysis and story style

Authors
Page 103

group starter questions for learning more information about story authors

Literature Group Evaluations

Self-Evaluation
Page 105

Group members each evaluate their own participation as well as the whole group's.

Leader Form
Page 106

The group leader uses the literature group record keeping form to evaluate the progress of each session.

Book-Share

The book ballot helps readers feel they have a choice in book selection. Many teachers track choices to ensure a first choice at least one out of three times.

Materials:
Book Ballot Page 152
5-7 copies of each book title
Pencil
Ballot box
Passages from 5 books

Goal:
To select the book you want to read and discuss in a literature group

Steps:
1. Listen as a passage from each book is read.
2. Mark your first, second and third book choice on the book ballot.
3. Place your ballot in the ballot box.

Just for Fun:
• Create your own book ballot.
• Design your own ballot box.
• Read a passage from your favorite book for the kids in your class.

Book Ballot Example

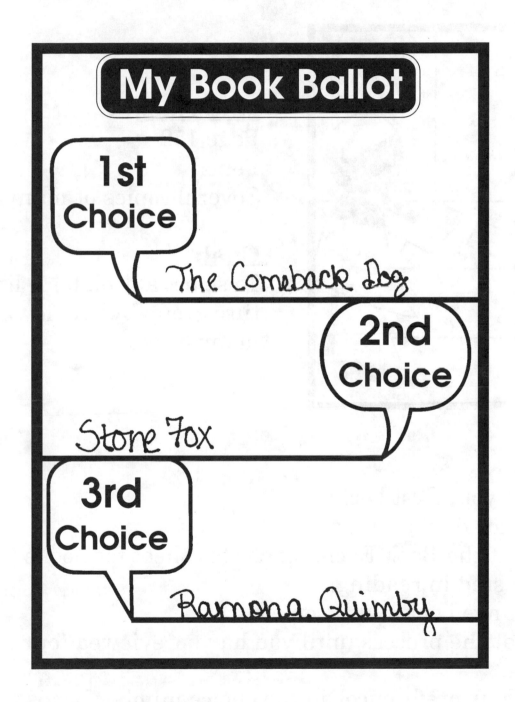

My Book Ballot

1st Choice

The Comeback Dog

2nd Choice

Stone Fox

3rd Choice

Ramona Quimby

Book Exchange

Readers really enjoy participating in a book exchange. It gives them an opportunity to preview a number of books. Many times they find new authors and titles for their Reading Idea List (page 33).

Materials:
Page 152
Pencil
Several copies of many books

Goal:
To select a book for a literature group by previewing many books.

Steps:
1. Select your first book.
2. Read for five minutes.
3. Fill out the Book Exchange Notes sheet for books you are interested in reading.
4. Exchange books with someone else.
5. Repeat the process until you have previewed four or five books.
6. List your preferences in the choice number boxes.

Just for Fun:
Design your own forms to list your choices.

Book Exchange Notes Example

Book Exchange Notes

Choice # 2

Book Title: The Lion, Witch and Wardrobe
Book Author: C.S. Lewis
Genre:
- ☑ Adventure
- ☐ Biography
- ☐ Fantasy
- ☐ Mystery
- ☐ Nonfiction
- ☐ Realistic Fiction
- ☐ Other:

My Interest Level: Low 1 • 2 • 3 • ④ • 5 High
Notes: I really liked this book

Choice # 1

Book Title: The Whipping Boy
Book Author: Sid Fleishman
Genre:
- ☐ Adventure
- ☐ Biography
- ☐ Fantasy
- ☐ Mystery
- ☐ Nonfiction
- ☐ Realistic Fiction
- ☑ Other: Humor

My Interest Level: Low 1 • 2 • 3 • 4 • ⑤ High
Notes: It's interesting and funny too.

Starting a Book Club Circle

Book Club Circles help younger readers share their book experience with others in a fun, nurturing environment. Adult leadership is necessary to model desired behavior. Circles can also focus on group members sharing their favorite books.

Materials:
5 copies of each book
Chairs in circle shape
Journal
Pencil

Goals:
To start a book club circle
To lead the first four
book club circles

Steps for first circle:
1. Sit in a circle (5 kids) with others reading the same book.
2. Share why you chose this book and/or what you think might happen in the story.
3. As a group, determine how many pages you will read by the next meeting (goal).

After your first circle:
1. Read your book.
2. Draw a picture or write a sentence in your journal about the story so far.
3. Bring your journal to the next meeting.

Book Club Starter Questions

Book Club Session 1. Starter Questions

1. What did you like about the cover of this book?
2. Why did you choose this book?
3. What do you think might happen in this story?

Book Club Session 2. Starter Questions

1. What did you notice about this book as you were reading it?
2. Would you like to share your journal drawing or writing?
3. How do you like the story so far? Why?

Book Club Session 3. Starter Questions

1. How did you feel when you were reading the story? (i.e. glad, happy, sad, mad)
2. Would you like to share your journal entry with us?
3. Who is your favorite character?

Book Club Session 4. Starter Questions

1. How does this story remind you of your life?
2. What is your favorite part of the story so far?
3. Please share your journal entry. Tell us about it.

Literature Group Focus: Genre

It helps to start a literature group by focusing on one genre and discussing its elements. Eventually, group members will eagerly discuss their books among themselves. Starter questions are springboards for future discussion.

Materials:
5-7 books (same genre)
Genre tree (p. 20)
Starter questions (p. 99)
Butcher paper

Goal:
To talk about the characteristics of a certain genre

Steps:
1. Meet in a group with other people reading a book of the same genre.
2. Brainstorm the elements found in the genre (e.g. Mystery: crime, suspense, climax). Write them onto butcher paper.
3. Share why you chose this book.
4. Discuss your favorite characteristics of this genre.
5. Determine together the focus for the next group meeting.

Just for Fun:
• Select another genre to focus on.
• Write your own series of starter questions.

Genre Starter Questions

Adventure

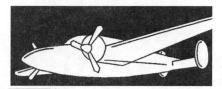

1. Briefly tell about the adventure in this story.
2. What parts of the adventure would you like to experience?
3. How would you change the adventure?

Biography

1. Who is the main character? Tell a little about him or her.
2. What new information have you learned about her/him?
3. Do you like this person? Please explain.

Fantasy/Fairytale

1. Where does this story take place?
2. Who is your favorite character? Why?
3. What is your favorite part of the story? Please explain.

Mystery

1. Was a crime committed in the story? If so, what was it?
2. Did the author do a good job building suspense? Please explain.
3. How would you change the mystery?

Historical

1. When does this story take place? Is it fiction or nonfiction?
2. Why were you interested in this time period?
3. Are you like any of the characters? How?

Realistic Fiction

1. Who are the main characters?
2. How does this story remind you of your life?
3. Do you think this story could really happen? Please explain.

Literature Group Focus: Story Elements

Story elements can be used as discussion starters in all types of literature groups. It helps to have an adult lead the group early on and then let the group follow its own direction.

Materials:
Five to seven copies of the same book
Starter questions (page 101)

Goal:
To discuss story elements in the same book

Steps for first group meeting:
1. Meet in a group with other people reading the same book.
2. Brainstorm the basic elements of any story (i.e. setting, plot, etc.).
3. Share what first attracted you to this book.
4. Predict what you think will happen in the story.
5. Determine the focus for your next group meeting.

Just for Fun:
Try creating your own group discussion starter questions and then watch how the discussion takes on a life of its own.

Story Element Starter Questions

Prediction

1. What clues does the book cover give you about the story?
2. After reading the first paragraph what do you predict will happen?
3. How does the author try to pull you into the story? Does it work?

Setting

1. Describe the setting of the story and the time period.
2. Does the setting remind you of anywhere you have been?
3. Do you think the setting fits the story? Why?

Characters

1. Who are the main characters?
2. Who is your favorite character? What makes this character your favorite?
3. What things do you have in common with the characters?

Plot

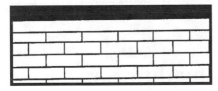

1. What problems do the characters face? How are they solved?
2. How would you solve these problems? Please explain.
3. Does this story plot remind you of any other story you've read?

Conclusion

1. Did the ending make sense to you? Why?
2. If you could change the ending, how would you change it?
3. If you could write a sequel, what would happen next?

Mood

1. Describe a scene in the book that made you laugh. What was funny?
2. Describe a sad scene. Did it remind you of anything you've experienced?
3. What was the most exciting part of the book? How did it make you feel?

Literature Group Focus: Authors

As readers compare and contrast the writing of different authors, they can integrate what they are learning into their own writing.

Materials:
Markers
Starter questions (page 103)
5-7 long rectangular strips of tagboard
5-7 books by different authors

Goal:
To compare the writing of different authors

Steps for first group:
1. Meet in a group of people reading books by different authors.
2. Write the first sentence in your book onto your strip of tagboard.
3. Each member shares his/her sentence with the rest of the group.
4. Discuss the differences and similarities in the first lines of each person's book. Do these lines make you want to read more? Does one line do this better than another? Why?
5. Determine the focus for your next group meeting.

Author Starter Questions

About this Author

1. What other books have you read by this author?

2. What do you know about this author?

3. How did you first learn about his/her books?

Genre

1. Does this author always write in the same genre?

2. Why do you think this author writes the books he/she does?

3. Do you like this person's writing? Please explain.

Research

1. Do you think this author does research to write his/her books?

2. What kinds of things did the author have to know to write this book?

3. How long do you think it would take to write this story?

Interest Level

1. Why did you choose to read this book?

2. How did the author capture your interest in the beginning of the story?

3. Has the author been able to keep you interested? How?

Language

1. Does the author do a good job of painting pictures with words?

2. What are your favorite parts?

3. Do you like the way the author describes the setting, characters and events? Give examples.

Story Line

1. Does the story make sense?

2. Has the author done a good job of explaining things in the story?

3. How would you change the way the story is written?

Evaluation Tools

Although literature groups take on many forms (structured and unstructured) they all present an opportunity to self-assess behavior and learning in a group setting. There is a literature group assesment tool for leaders on page 106.

Materials:
Page 153
Pencil/pen

Goals:
To assess group goals
To assess and record individual goals

Steps:
1. Think about today's session.
2. Leaders fill out the form on page 154 as members fill out the form on page 153.
3. Each member states his/her group rating (1-5) and personal rating (1-5) as the leader records this information as well as each member's personal goal.
4. Leader rates each student and explains his or her rating.
5. The group works together to identify new goals and decides on a group score for the week.

Just for Fun:
Create your own evaluation forms.

Self-Evaluation Form

My Name: Danielle

My Literature Circle Assessment Form

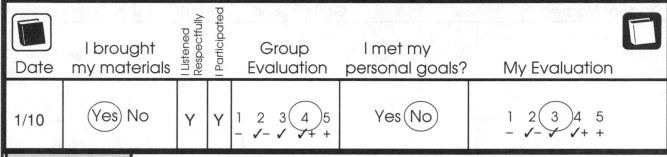

Date	I brought my materials	I Listened Respectfully	I Participated	Group Evaluation	I met my personal goals?	My Evaluation
1/10	(Yes) No	Y	Y	1 2 3 (4) 5 – ✓– ✓ ✓+ +	Yes (No)	1 2 (3) 4 5 – ✓– ✓ ✓+ +

Next Week's Assignmnent:	To read to page 62 and write the things that are similar in my life to
Brian's.	

My Personal Goal:	To bring my book next week and talk more.

NOTES

We had fun talking about Brian's adventure and if we were going to be stranded somewhere what would we want to have with us so we would be OK.

Leader's Name: **Michelle**   Date: **2–10**

Book Title: **Hatchet**

Literature Circle Leader Evaluation Form

How did we do?

1	2	3	4	5
–	✓–	✓	✓+	+

Group score — Participation 4 / Materials 4

Student Name	Brought Materials (Y/N)	Read Book (Y/N)	Listened Respectfully (Scale)	Participated (Scale)	Student Rating — Group	Self	Leader Rating — Student	Student Met Personal Goal (Y/N)	New Goal
Matt P.	Y	Y	4	3	4	4	4	Y	talk more
Cheryl N.	Y	Y	5	4	4	4	4+	Y	talk more
Jeff S.	N	Y	3	5	4+	3	3+	N	> respectful
Hannah J.	Y	N	4	4	5	3	3+	Y	bring pencils
Megan O.	Y	Y	4	4	5	5	5	Y	not read past page
Steven F.	N	Y	3	3	4	2	3	N	talk more

Comments: Group excited about the book, the descriptive language and the survival skills they are learning through Gary Paulsen's story. They are building group process skills, but it is still hard for them to hold back when another member is talking. Each of the students are working on their personal goals and group goals.

The group is getting more cohesive each session. *Matt* talked more this session, but wants to participate a bit more, *Cheryl* is still shy, but is getting more chatty now, *Jeff* is working on respectful listening - he just gets so excited about things that he has trouble not interrupting, *Hannah* was embarrassed because she forgot to read - I don't think she will do that again, *Megan* - as always is right on target and a group leader, and *Steven* has decided that he really likes this book - that will help him.

Assignments:

Chapter 6

Fun Reading Projects

Fun Reading Projects

"My favorite reading project is a Wanted Poster. It's fun making up what the people did right or wrong and it's fun drawing."
Kelsey Holt, 5th grade

Readers are inspired in different ways by the stories they've read. Reading a good book can be very energizing. It's fun to use that energy to create something that symbolizes what we've read. It's a wonderful opportunity to extend our reading experience.

The reading projects in this chapter are based upon the recommendations of other kids. They were asked to share their classroom favorites with *Beyond Book Reports* readers. The projects that are included in this chapter are those they felt were the most fun to create and share with others. Each project has been kid-tested and approved.

We hope you enjoy these projects. **Have fun creating your own reading projects!**

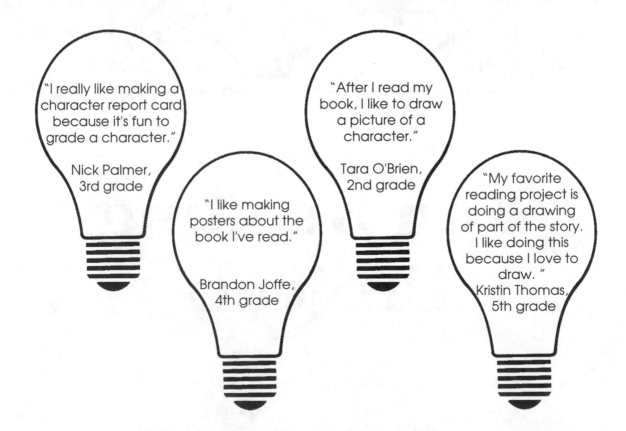

"I really like making a character report card because it's fun to grade a character."

Nick Palmer, 3rd grade

"I like making posters about the book I've read."

Brandon Joffe, 4th grade

"After I read my book, I like to draw a picture of a character."

Tara O'Brien, 2nd grade

"My favorite reading project is doing a drawing of part of the story. I like doing this because I love to draw."
Kristin Thomas, 5th grade

About This Chapter

This chapter includes...

Reading Project List

The Reading Project List on page 155, includes the name and page number of twenty reading projects listed throughout *Beyond Book Reports*. It provides readers who are interested in doing a reading project with ideas and a place to record a completed project.

Projects in this Chapter

The projects in this chapter help readers synthesize and apply what they have learned from the books they've read. The following projects are included:

Special Bookmarks	*Page 112*
Puppet Characters	*Page 114*
Character Report Card	*Page 116*
Story Cube	*Page 118*
Story Quilt	*Page 120*
Character Mask	*Page 122*
Character Wanted Poster	*Page 124*
3-D Setting Map	*Page 126*
Advertise-a-Book Poster	*Page 128*

The Project Supply Sheet on page 130, helps readers organize their project materials.

Reading Project List

The Reading Project List helps readers keep track of the various projects they've already completed. It also helps them select a reading project. The Project Supply Sheet on page 130 will help readers organize their projects.

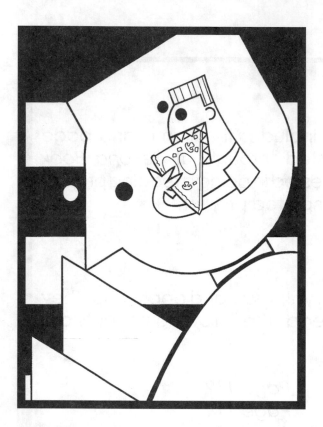

Materials:
Page 155
Pencil/pen

Goals:
To help you select a project

To record the projects you've completed and their book titles

Steps:
1. Use the project list to select your project.
2. Look up the directions on the page given.
3. Mark an X in the project box after you complete your project.
4. Write the title of the book and the completion date as shown on page 111.
5. Place a star by a project you especially liked.
6. Add some of your favorite projects to the bottom of the list.

Just for Fun:
- Make your own reading project list.
- Make a classroom reading project list out of butcher paper.

Reading Project List Example

Page	Reading Project	Helen Keller 1-8-93	Castle in Attic 2-35-93				
42	Author Profile						
128	Advertise-a-Book Poster						
112	Bookmark						
74	Book-Sell						
76	Book-Talk						
88	Bubble Gum Review						
122	Character Mask						
116	Character Report Card						
44	Illustrator Profile						
40	Letter to an Author						
86	Pizza Report						
114	Puppet Character						
82	Remarkable Review						
126	3-D Setting Map						
118	Story Cube						
57	Story Map (Individual)						
58	Story Map (Group)						
120	Story Quilt						
69	Venn Diagram						
124	Character Wanted Poster						
___	_____						
___	_____						
___	_____						
___	_____						
___	_____						

Bookmarks

This project is great for new readers. It makes reading their special book even more fun. After the bookmark is finished you can make it more durable by covering it with clear contact paper or laminating it.

Materials:
Page 156
Scissors
Popsicle sticks/ribbon
Glue
Crayons/marker/pencil
Tagboard/Paper

Goal:
To create a special bookmark for the book you are reading

Steps:
1. Decide on the design of your bookmark. There are some examples on page 113.
2. Draw the shape onto tagboard/cardboard.
3. Cut out the shape and draw your design.
4. Glue a popsicle stick, ribbon or strip of paper to the back if you want to make it longer.

Just for Fun:
Make a bookmark as a gift for someone who might like the book.

Bookmark Examples

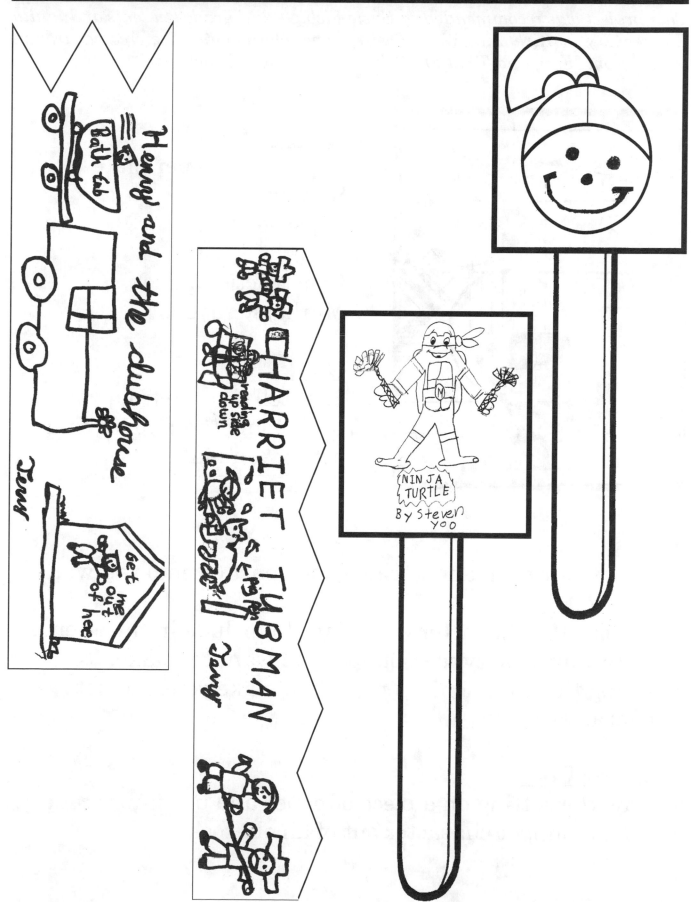

Puppet Characters

This project was recommended by Suzie Fiebig's 2nd-grade students at Juanita Elementary in Kirkland, WA. Their puppet characters were created around scenes from "Frog and Toad are Friends," by Arnold Lobel.

Materials:
Paper sack/paper plate
Scissors
Popsicle sticks
Glue
Construction paper
Markers/crayons

Goal:
To retell a scene from your book using the puppet characters you make

Steps:
1. Read your book and decide which part (scene) you want to retell.
2. Choose the characters you want to include in this scene.
3. Determine the type of puppet you want to make.
4. Using the directions on page 115, make your puppet character(s).

Just for Fun:
- Draw the setting on a piece of paper and use it for scenery.
- Make a puppet character out of an old sock.

Puppet Character Directions

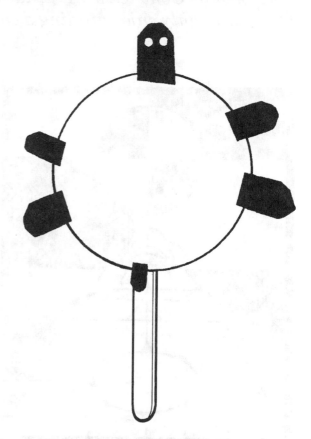

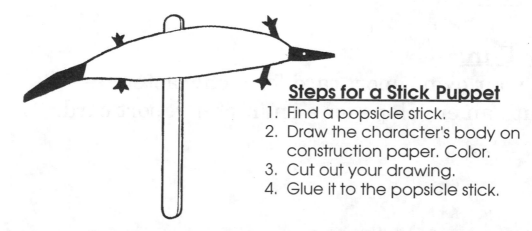

Steps for a Sack Puppet

1. Find a small paper sack.
2. Draw the character's arms, legs, head, and top and bottom lips on paper. Color them.
3. Cut out each of your drawings.
4. Glue them onto the bag as shown above.
5. Put your hand inside the bag and move your character's lips as you talk for it.

Steps for a Plate Puppet

1. Find a popsicle stick and paper plate.
2. Draw the character's arms, legs, head (tail if it needs one) onto construction paper. Color them.
3. Cut out each of your drawings.
4. Glue them onto the outside of a paper plate as shown above.
5. Glue a popsicle stick to the inside of the plate.

Steps for a Stick Puppet

1. Find a popsicle stick.
2. Draw the character's body on construction paper. Color.
3. Cut out your drawing.
4. Glue it to the popsicle stick.

Character Report Card

Lori Blevins Gonwick's 3rd-grade students at Juanita Elementary in Kirkland, WA, thoroughly enjoy grading a character in a story and heartily recommend it.

Materials:
Page 157
Pencil/markers

Goal:
To write a report card for a character in the book you are reading

Steps:
1. Read your book.
2. Choose the character for the report card.
3. Grade the character on his/her behavior in the story.
4. Write in comments to describe why the character earned this grade.

Just for Fun:
- Create your own report card for a character.
- Illustrate an envelope for a character report card.

Report Card Example

Character Report Card

Character

E	Outstanding	
S+	Good	
S	Satisfactory	
S-	Needs improving	
N	Needs to try again	

Student: Kimi

Teacher: Steven Yoo

Grade: 4th grade

"It's the Soup that Made Me Sad"

Book Title

BEHAVIOR	GRADE	COMMENTS
Positive attitude:	S-	Because she didn't clean up her room up.
Follows directions:	S-	
Helpful:	S	She was nice to a man in a
Thoughtfulness of others:	S+	restrong.
Pays attention:	N	She couldn't find her baseball mitt.
Assumes and carries through responsibilities:	S+	She improved when she cleaned up her room.
Other Comments:		

Story Cube

There are many ways to share a story cube. The focus can be on story characters, plot, story scenes etc. Small boxes can also be purchased at art supply stores.

Materials:
Tagboard
Markers/pencil/crayons
Scissors
Glue

Goal:
To retell a story using the drawings and information on the story cube

Steps:

1. Determine the size of your story cube and trace six square panels onto tagboard in the shape shown on the next page. Cut your cube out.
2. Select the story you want to retell with your box. Decide what you want to draw and/or write on the outside of your cube. Draw and write on each square. Note: panels 1,2, and 6, are drawn straight. Panels 3,4, and 5, are drawn facing out (see example on the next page).
3. Fold the cube panels as shown and glue them together.
4. Share your special story cube with friends.

Story Cube Directions

Step 1

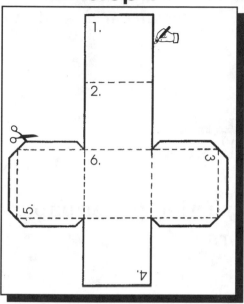

Trace your box onto tagboard
and cut it out.

Step 2

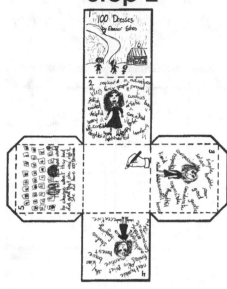

Draw and write the things you want to
share from the story in each square.
Note the direction each square's drawing is facing.

Step 3

Turn the illustrated side over and fold it
into a box shape (as shown above).
Glue each square edge to another.

Step 4

Erin's Book Box for
One Hundred Dresses
by Eleanor Estes

After the glue dries you can share
your story cube with your friends.

Story Quilt

The Story Quilt was recommended by Valerie Marshall and Martha Ivy's 4th-grade students at McAuliffe Elementary in Redmond, WA. Students take turns illustrating a scene. By the end of the book, they have created a class story quilt.

Materials:
Pencil/markers
Glue
Construction paper/paper
Scissors

Goal:
To share a book through a drawn quilt made up of scenes from a favorite story

Steps:
1. Read your book.
2. Reread your favorite scenes.
3. Decide how many pieces you will include in your story quilt.
4. List the scenes you want to include.
5. Draw each scene onto the same size paper.
6. Use a construction paper border around the outside of the quilt and between the quilt pieces.
7. Retell the story using the pictures from your story quilt.

Just for Fun:
Paint a story quilt and put it up in your school library

Story Quilt Example

The Master Puppeteer
by
Katherine Paterson

Story Quilt by Juleah Swanson

Making a Character Mask

Valerie Marshall and Martha Ivy's 4th-graders filled their room with character masks hanging in a row. This is a great recycling project.

Materials:
Pantyhose leg (used)
Yarn/ribbon
Hanger (wire)
Construction paper
Markers/crayons
Glue

Goal:
To create a mask of a character in the book you are reading

Steps:
1. Stretch out the bottom of the wire hanger.
2. Slip the pantyhose around the hanger and tie it at the top with yarn.
3. Cut yarn or ribbon for hair and glue it to the mask.
4. Draw and cut paper eyes, nose and mouth.
5. Glue these onto the mask and hang it up for everyone to see.

Just for Fun:
• Take turns guessing who each character mask represents.
• Use different colored and textured pantyhose to get just the right look for a mask.

Character Mask Directions

Step 1

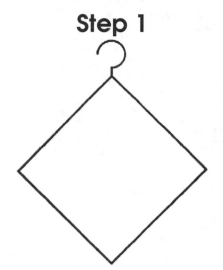

Stretch out a hanger by pulling down on the bottom.

Step 2

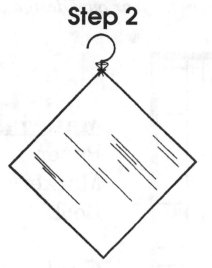

Slip pantyhose leg around hanger and tie at the top.

Step 3

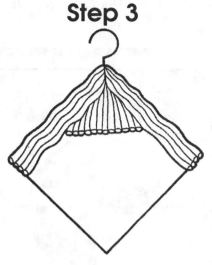

Cut yarn or ribbon for hair and glue to the mask.

Step 4

Draw eyes, nose, and mouth onto construction paper. Cut them out.

Step 5

Glue the face pieces onto your character mask.

Character Masks

Hang your mask up with others and guess who the characters are.

Character Wanted Poster

Japhy Whalen's 4th- and 5th-grade students at Graham Hill Elementary in Seattle, WA, recommend the 3-D Character Wanted Poster as their favorite reading project. It's fun to create your own design and layout.

Materials:
Paper
Marker/pencil
Book

Goal:
To create a wanted poster of your character to share with your friends

Steps:

1. Decide upon the character for your wanted poster.
2. Think about how you want your poster to look and what you want to say on it.
3. Using the information you've learned about the character in the story, draw a picture in the center of the page.
4. Write in the information you've chosen to include and draw an outside border.

Just for Fun:

Make your poster using pictures and letters from magazines.

Wanted Poster Example

Moon Shadow

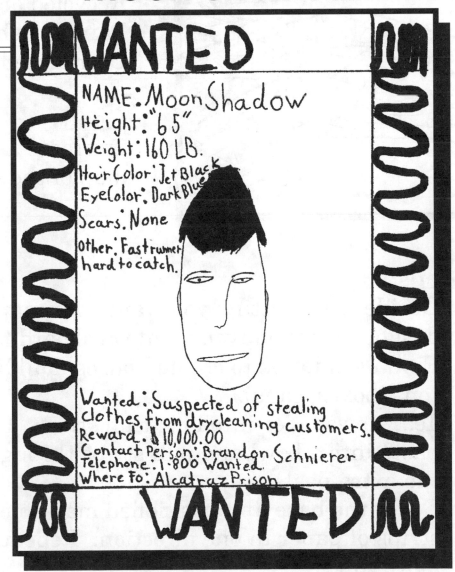

Wanted Poster by Brian Schnierer

3-D Setting Map

Joyce Standing's 5th-grade class at the Overlake School in Redmond, WA, recommends the 3-D Setting Map as a great reading project. It's fun, it's messy, and kids thoroughly enjoy creating a lasting work of art.

Materials:
Old newspapers
Tempera paint
Wallpaper paste
Recycled objects
Paint brush
Corrugated cardboard

Goal:
To create a 3-dimensional map of the story

Steps:
1. Decide what setting you want your map to represent and design the map layout. Cut cardboard for the map base.
2. Find used items to create houses, buildings, etc. (milk cartons, boxes, cans).
3. Tear newspaper into long thin strips. Pour wallpaper paste into a bowl and pull strips through it, squeezing off the extra paste.
4. Cover the base and positioned map objects by layering strips of paper in one direction. Repeat this process four more times
5. When dry (1-2 days), paint objects and base.

3-D Setting Map Directions

Step 1

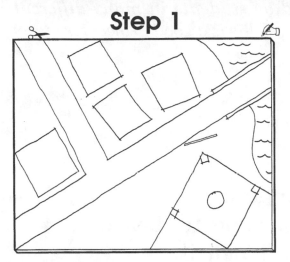

Design the layout of your setting map. Cut cardboard to create the base of your map.

Step 2

Collect used items for your setting. Small milk cartons, boxes, cans and other household items work well.

Step 3

Tear newspaper into long thin strips. Pour wallpaper paste in a bowl and pull strips through, squeezing off any extra paste.

Step 4

Laying strips in the same direction, cover the base and objects.

Repeat this step four or more times and let dry.

Step 5

Paint the base and the objects on your map. Share it with others.

Advertise-a-Book Poster

An Advertise-a-Book Poster was recommended by students in many different classrooms. Its creative possibilities are limitless. This is a good project for many different grade levels.

Materials:
Tagboard/poster board
Markers/pencil

Goal:
To create a poster that will make people want to read your book

Steps:
1. Decide which book you want to advertise.
2. Think about the most interesting parts of the story.
3. Lay out your ideas on a piece of paper.
4. Later, come back to your poster design ideas and change anything that doesn't fit.
5. Draw your poster onto tagboard.

Just for Fun:
• Make a collage out of magazine photographs
• Use computer graphics to create your poster

Advertise-a-Book Poster Example

Shrink into
"The Castle in the Attic"
for...

Adventure

Excitement

Suspense

Book by Elizabeth Winthrop
Poster by Nick

Project Supply Sheet Example

My Project Supply Sheet

Name: *Nick*

My Project is: Advertise-a-book Poster

To do my project I will need:

Writing Tools
- ✓ pencil(s)
- ✓ marker(s)
- ___ pen(s)
- ✓ crayons
- ___

Art Supplies
- ___ glue
- ___ paste
- ___ wallpaper paste
- ✓ scissors
- ___ paint
- ___ paint brush
- ___ glitter
- ___ stickers
- ___ tape
- ___

Paper Supplies
- ___ form (page #   )
- ___ plain paper
- ___ lined paper
- ___ construction paper
- ✓ tagboard
- ___ butcher paper
- ___ newspaper
- ___ cardboard
- ___ corrugated cardboard
- ___ contact paper
- ___

Other Possible Items
- ✓ book
- ___ popsicle stick
- ___ paper sack
- ___ ribbon
- ___ yarn
- ___ envelope
- ___ stamp
- ___ video camera
- ___ pantyhose
- ___ hanger
- ___ recycled objects
- ___

Chapter 7

Reference Books

Reference Books

Author	Book Title	Publisher
Brown, Hazel Cambourne, Brian	*Read and Retell*	Heinemann Educational Books, 1990
Calkins, Lucy McCormick	*Lessons from a Child*	Heinemann Educational Books, 1983
Hornsby, David Sukarna, Deborah Parry, Jo-Ann	*Read On: A Conference Approach to Reading*	Heinemann Educational Books, 1986
Johnson, Terry D. Louis, Daphne R.	*Literacy through Literature*	Heinemann Educational Books, 1987
Norton, Donna	*The Impact of Literature Based Reading*	HarperCollins Publishers, 1990
O'Brien-Palmer, Michelle	*Great Graphic Organizers To Use With Any Book!*	Scholastic Professional Books, 1997
Peterson, Ralph Eeds, Maryann	*Grand Conversations: Literature Groups in Action*	Scholastic, 1990
Rothlein, Liz Meinbach, Anita Meyer	*The Literature Connection*	Scott, Foresman and Company, 1991
Routman, Reggie	*Invitations*	Heinemann Educational Books, 1991
Samway, Katharine Davies Whang, Gail	*Literature Study Circles in a Multicultural Classroom*	Stenhouse Publishers, 1996
Short, Kathy Pierce, Katherine	*Talking About Books*	Heinemann Educational Books, 1990

Chapter 8

Forms to Copy

Interest Sheet

1. Things I like to do at home

2. Things I really like to do at school

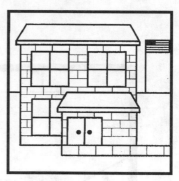

3. My favorite movies, videos & TV shows

Book Ideas

1._____

_____

_____

2._____

_____

_____

3._____

_____

_____

4._____

_____

_____

4. Things I wonder about

Name:

Books I Really Want To Read!

Title	Author	Genre	I read it! ✓

My Reading Record

Name:

Date	Book Title	Page

Beyond Book Reports Scholastic Inc

Genre Pizza Toppings

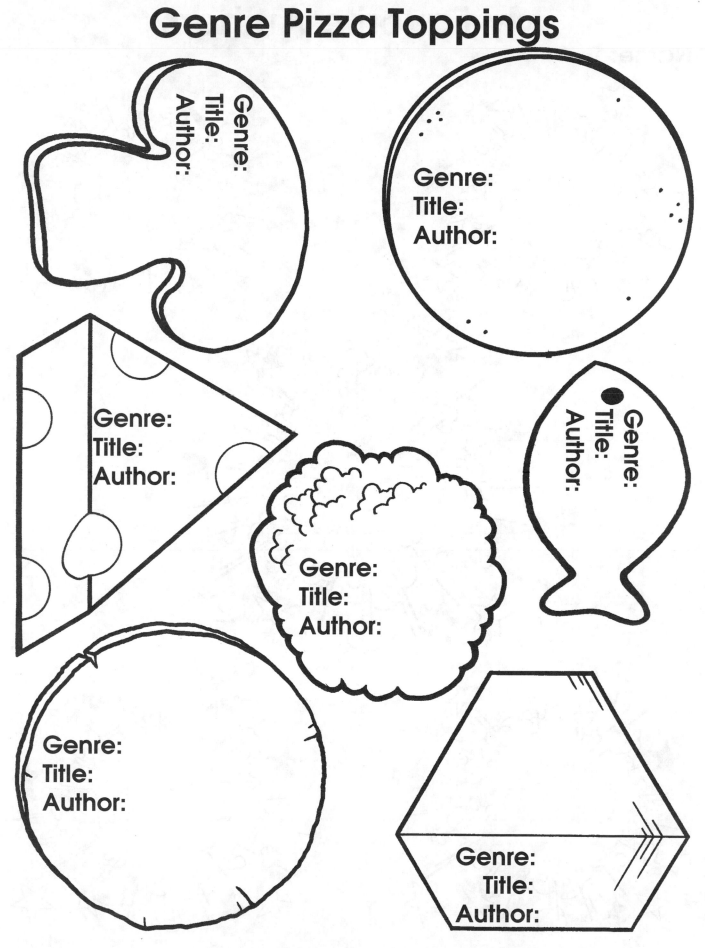

Genre:
Title:
Author:

Genre:
Title:
Author:

Genre:
Title:
Author:

Genre:
Title:
Author:

Genre:
Title:
Author:

Genre:
Title:
Author:

Genre:
Title:
Author:

My Favorite Authors

Name:

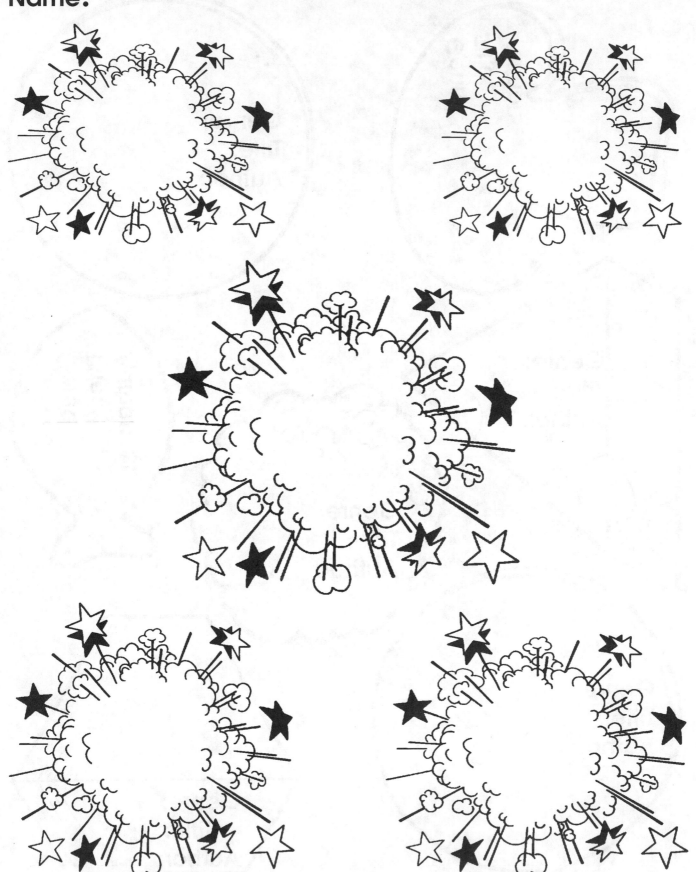

Author Profile

Name:

Author's name, age
and home

Author's family

Number of books written
and some book titles

Favorite type of writing

Why author likes to write

Illustrator Profile

Name:

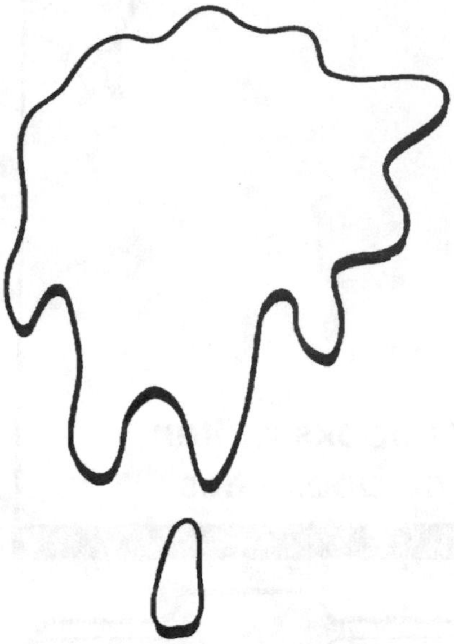

Illustrator's name
and age

Illustrator's home

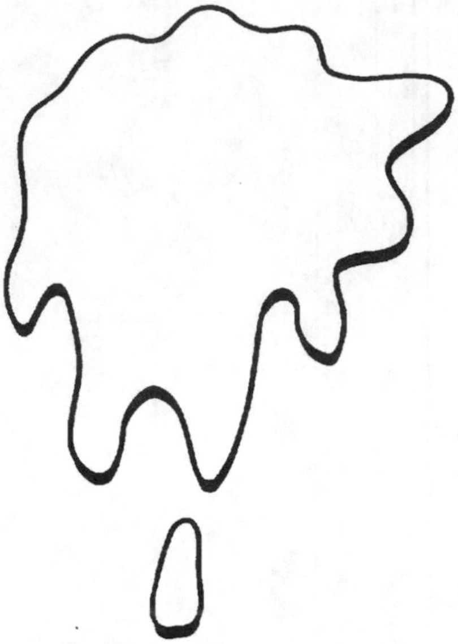

Illustrator's family

Number of books illustrated
and some titles

Favorite type of art

Why illustrator draws

My Favorite Illustrators

Name:

Name:

Story Sheet
Things I noticed in the story

Beginning   **Middle**   **End**

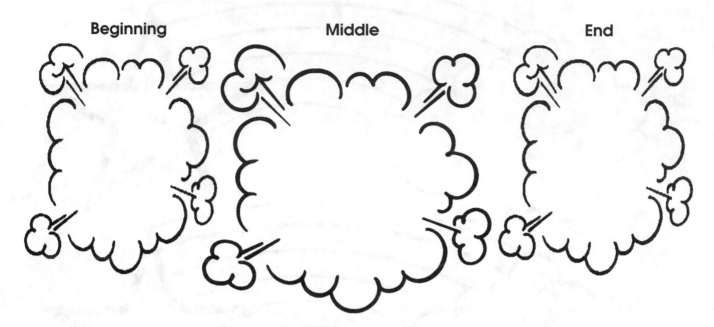

My Feelings
(Circle the feelings)

How this story reminds me of my life

Story Map

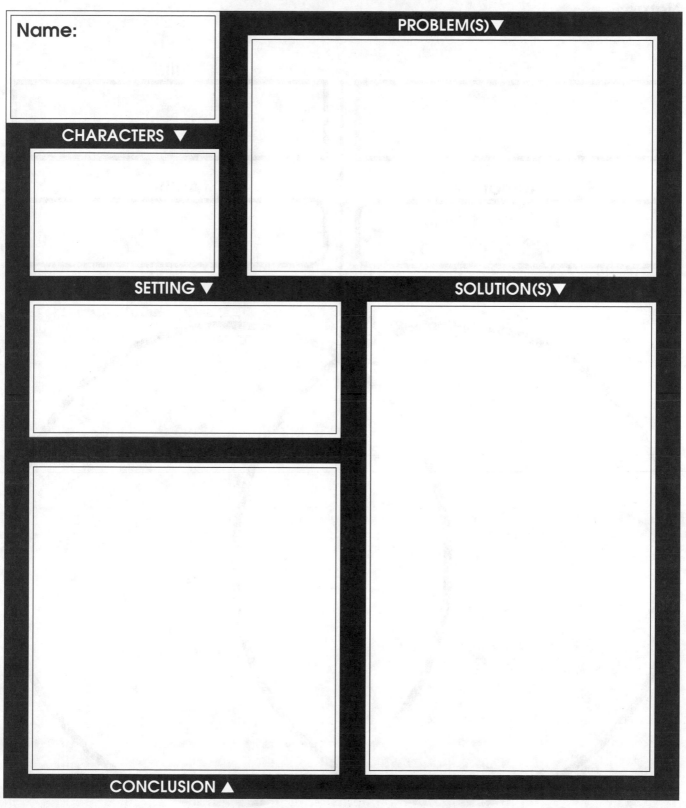

Name:

PROBLEM(S) ▼

CHARACTERS ▼

SETTING ▼

SOLUTION(S) ▼

CONCLUSION ▲

Venn Diagram

Name:

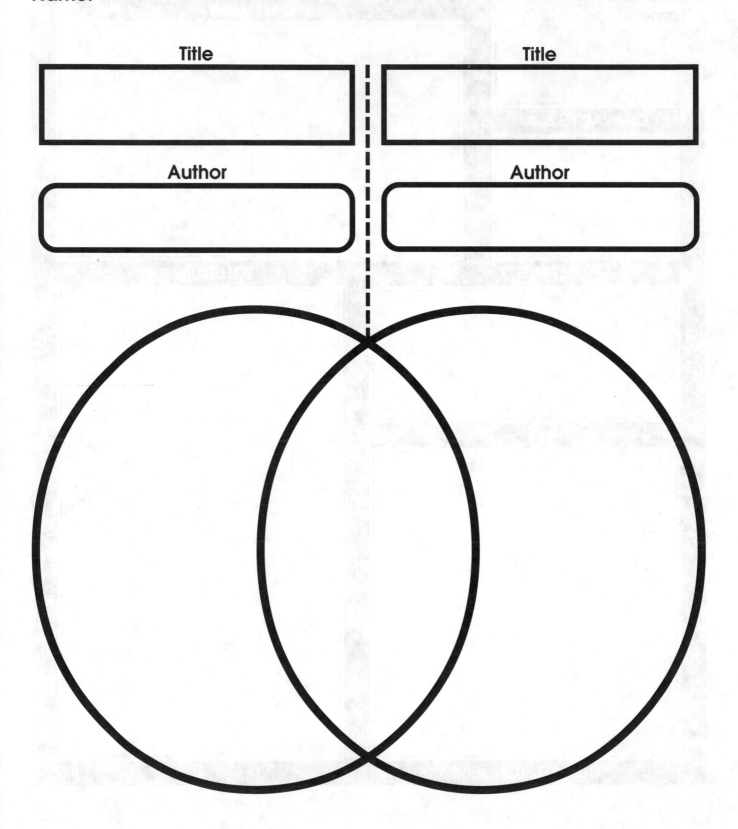

| Title | Title |

| Author | Author |

Character Comparison Sheet

Name:

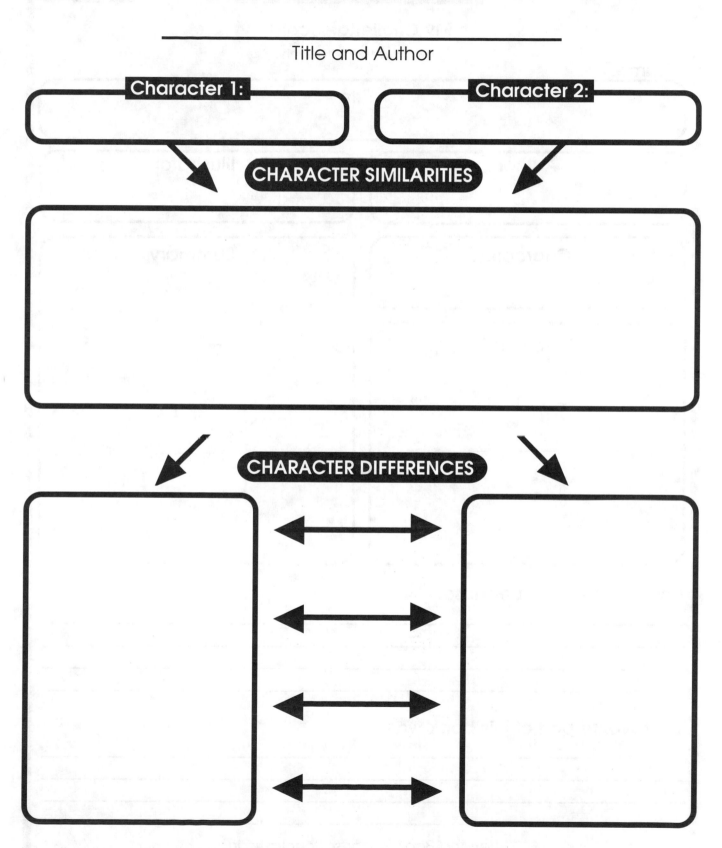

Title and Author

Character 1:

Character 2:

CHARACTER SIMILARITIES

CHARACTER DIFFERENCES

Beyond Book Reports Scholastic Inc

Remarkable Reviewer

This Book's HOT!

My Challenge Scale

Low **1•2•3•4•5** High

Name:

Title

Author

Illustrator

Characters

Summary

Setting

I chose this book because:

_____

_____

_____

_____

My favorite part of this book was:

_____

_____

_____

_____

Remarkable Reviewer

This Book's OK

My Challenge Scale
Low 1•2•3•4•5 High

Name:

Title

Author

Illustrator

Characters

Summary

Setting

I chose this book because:

_____

The reason I think this book is just OK is:

_____
_____
_____

I would recommend it to a friend: YES ☐ NO ☐

Please explain:_____
_____
_____

Beyond Book Reports Scholastic Inc

Remarkable Reviewer

This Book's NOT HOT!

My Challenge Scale
Low 1•2•3•4•5 High

Name:

| Title |

| Author | | Illustrator |

| Characters | | Summary |

| Setting | |

I chose this book because:

_____
_____
_____
_____

I didn't like this book because:

_____
_____
_____
_____

Pizza Reports

Canadian Bacon Report

_____
Title of the book

Author_____

Illustrator_____

# of pages____

easy❏ medium❏ challenge❏

Where does the story take place?

_____

_____

_____

Do you recommend this book? Y N

**Draw a picture of
the setting on the back**

Sausage Report

Title _____

Author_____

Illustrator_____

# of pages___ easy❏ medium❏ challenge❏

What happens at the beginning of the story?

_____

_____

What happens in the middle of the story?

_____

_____

What happens at the end of the story?

_____

_____

Do you like the ending?
Yes ❏ No ❏

Anchovy Report

Title_____

Author_____

Illustrator_____

pages___   Easy❑ Medium❑ Challenge❑

Write a paragraph about the story. Be sure to talk about the characters, setting and ending. _____

_____

_____

_____

Do you recommend this book?

Yes ❑ No ❑

Pepperoni Report

Title_____

Author_____

Illustrator_____

# of pages___   easy❑ medium❑ challenge❑

What is the "Main Character's" goal?

_____

Do you like the "Main Character"? Why?

_____

_____

If you were the "Main Character" what other ways would you try to reach the goal?

_____

_____

_____

_____

_____

Rewrite the ending on the back

Bubble Gum Review

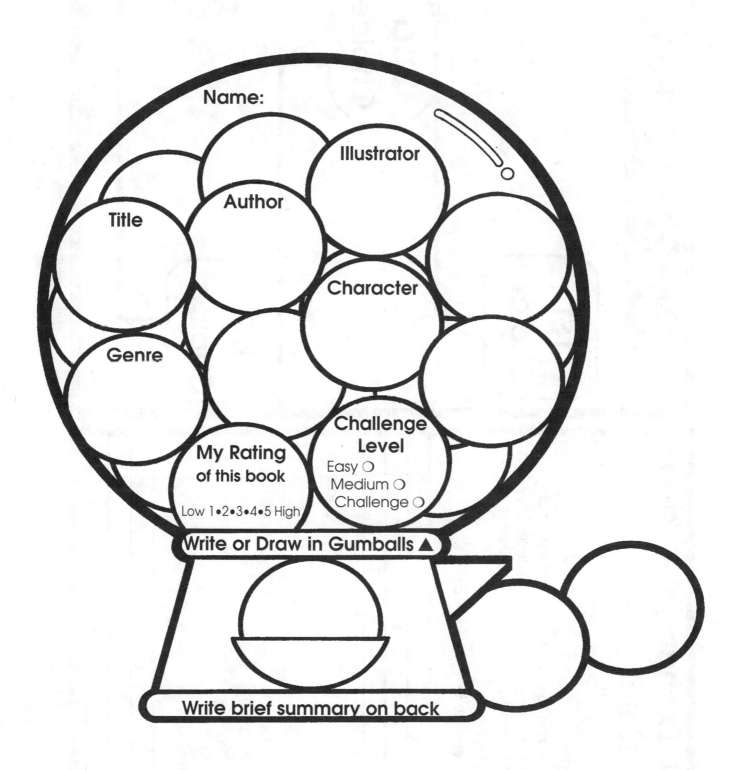

Name:

Illustrator

Author

Title

Character

Genre

Challenge Level
Easy ○
Medium ○
Challenge ○

My Rating of this book

Low 1•2•3•4•5 High

Write or Draw in Gumballs ▲

Write brief summary on back

Beyond Book Reports Scholastic Inc

Book Ballot and Book Exchange Notes

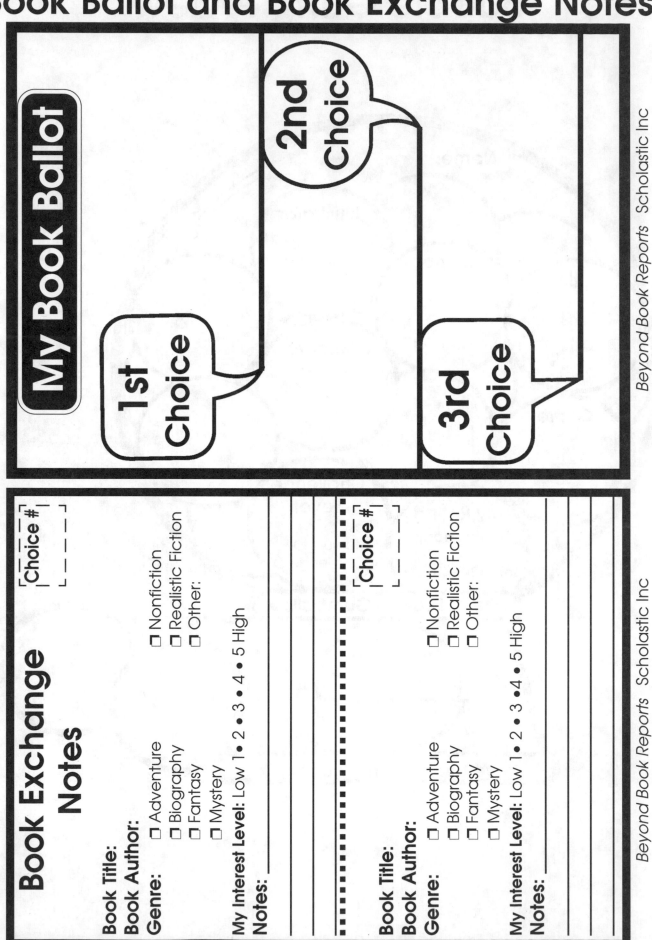

My Book Book Ballot

1st Choice

2nd Choice

3rd Choice

Book Exchange Notes

Choice #___

Book Title:
Book Author:
Genre: ☐ Adventure ☐ Nonfiction
☐ Biography ☐ Realistic Fiction
☐ Fantasy ☐ Other:
☐ Mystery

My Interest Level: Low 1 • 2 • 3 • 4 • 5 High
Notes:

Choice #___

Book Title:
Book Author:
Genre: ☐ Adventure ☐ Nonfiction
☐ Biography ☐ Realistic Fiction
☐ Fantasy ☐ Other:
☐ Mystery

My Interest Level: Low 1 • 2 • 3 •4 • 5 High
Notes:

My Literature Circle Assessment Form

My Name:_____

Date	I brought my materials	I Listened Respectfully	I Participated	Group Evaluation	I met my personal goals?	My Evaluation
	Yes No			1 2 3 4 5 – ✓– ✓ ✓+ +	Yes No	1 2 3 4 5 – ✓– ✓ ✓+ +

Next Week's Assignmnent:	

My Personal Goal:	

Forms from Book-Talk: a Scholastic Professional Book

My Literature Circle Assessment Form

My Name:_____

Date	I brought my materials	I Listened Respectfully	I Participated	Group Evaluation	I met my personal goals?	My Evaluation
	Yes No			1 2 3 4 5 – ✓– ✓ ✓+ +	Yes No	1 2 3 4 5 – ✓– ✓ ✓+ +

Next Week's Assignmnent:	

My Personal Goal:	

Leader's Name:_____ Date:_____
Book Title:_____

Literature Circle Leader Evaluation Form

	Y/N		Scale ●◇		How did we do? 1 2 3 4 5 − ✓− ✓ ✓+ +			Y/N	Group score Participation ☐ Materials
Student Name	Brought Materials	Read Book	Listened Respectfully	Participated	**Student Rating** Group Self		**Leader Rating** Student	Student Met Personal Goal	New Goal
					☐ ☐		☐	___	___
					☐ ☐		☐	___	___
					☐ ☐		☐	___	___
					☐ ☐		☐	___	___
					☐ ☐		☐	___	___
					☐ ☐		☐	___	___
					☐ ☐		☐	___	___
					☐ ☐		☐	___	___
					☐ ☐		☐	___	___
					☐ ☐		☐	___	___

Comments:

Assignments:

Reading Project List

Page	Reading Activity						
42	Author Profile						
129	Advertise-a-Book Poster						
112	Bookmark						
74	Book-Sell						
76	Book-Talk						
88	Bubble Gum Review						
122	Character Mask						
116	Character Report Card						
44	Illustrator Profile						
40	Letter to an Author						
86	Pizza Report						
114	Puppet Character						
82	Remarkable Review						
126	Setting Map						
118	Story Cube						
57	Story Map (Individual)						
58	Story Map (Group)						
120	Story Quilt						
69	Venn Diagram						
124	Wanted Poster						

Bookmark Templates

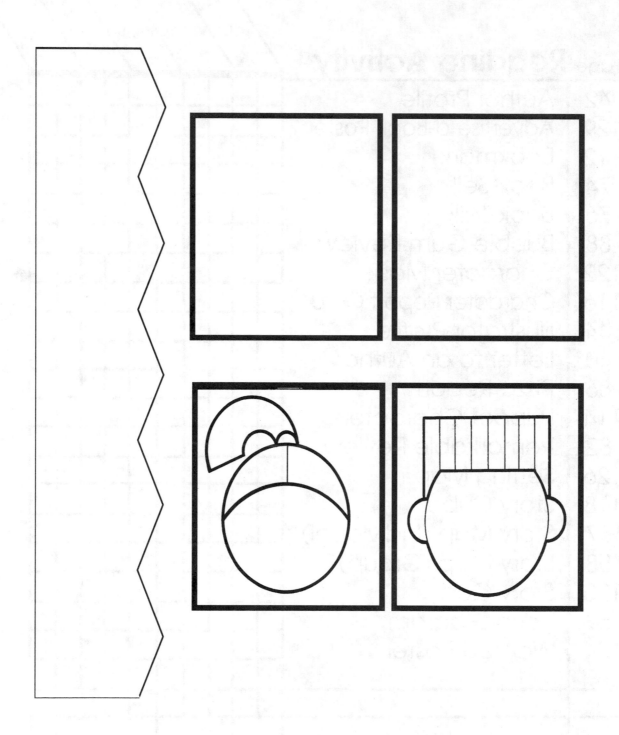

Beyond Book Reports Scholastic Inc

Character Report Card

Character

E	Outstanding
S+	Good
S	Satisfactory
S-	Needs improving
N	Needs to try again

Student: _____

Teacher: _____

Grade: _____

_____
Book Title

BEHAVIOR	GRADE	COMMENTS
Positive attitude:	_____	_____
Follows directions:	_____	_____
Helpful: Thoughtfulness of others:	_____	_____
Pays attention:	_____	_____
Assumes and carries through responsibilities:	_____	_____
Other Comments:	_____

_____
_____
_____
_____

✿ My Project Supply Sheet

Name: _____

My Project is: _____

To do my project I will need:

Writing Tools
___ pencil(s)
___ marker(s)
___ pen(s)
___ crayons

Art Supplies
___ glue
___ paste
___ wallpaper paste
___ scissors
___ paint
___ paint brush
___ glitter
___ stickers
___ tape

Paper Supplies
___ form :page #
___ plain paper
___ lined paper
___ construction paper
___ tagboard
___ butcher paper
___ newspaper
___ cardboard
___ corrugated cardboard
___ contact paper

Other Possible Items
___ book
___ popsicle stick
___ paper sack
___ ribbon
___ yarn
___ envelope
___ stamp
___ video camera
___ pantyhose
___ hanger
___ recycled objects

Beyond Book Reports Scholastic Inc

✿ My Project Supply Sheet

Name: _____

My Project is: _____

To do my project I will need:

Writing Tools
___ pencil(s)
___ marker(s)
___ pen(s)
___ crayons

Art Supplies
___ glue
___ paste
___ wallpaper paste
___ scissors
___ paint
___ paint brush
___ glitter
___ stickers
___ tape

Paper Supplies
___ form :page #
___ plain paper
___ lined paper
___ construction paper
___ tagboard
___ butcher paper
___ newspaper
___ cardboard
___ corrugated cardboard
___ contact paper

Other Possible Items
___ book
___ popsicle stick
___ paper sack
___ ribbon
___ yarn
___ envelope
___ stamp
___ video camera
___ pantyhose
___ hanger
___ recycled objects

Beyond Book Reports Scholastic Inc

ABOUT THE AUTHOR
Of...

BOOK-WRITE

BEYOND BOOK REPORTS

**GREAT GRAPHIC ORGANIZERS TO USE WITH
ANY BOOK !**

Michelle received her undergraduate and graduate degrees at the University of Washington. Her career in educational curriculum development and design spans twenty years.

Michelle works with students and teachers in five to six different classrooms for seven months as she proceeds through the writing of each of her books. Children and classroom teachers always play an integral role in the creation of of her books and music.

- *Educational Workshops and Inservices*
- *School Assemblies and Workshops*
- *Educational Consultation*

MicNik Publications, Inc.• P.O. Box 3041
Kirkland, Washington 98072 • (425) 881-6476